TALES
OF THE
ENLIGHTENED

TALES
OF
THE ENLIGHTENED

by
DR. S. Z. KAHANA

Speculations on
Legendary Phenomena
by the Hans Christian
Anderson of Israel

RESEARCH CENTRE OF KABBALAH
JERUSALEM — NEW YORK

ISBN: Hard Cover 0-943688-39-6
ISBN: Soft Cover 0-943688-40-X

For further information address:
Research Centre of Kabbalah
P.O. Box 14168
The Old City, Jerusalem, Israel
or
The Research Centre of Kabbalah
200 Park Ave. Suite 303E
New York, N.Y. 10017

Printed in the U.S.A.
1985

TABLE OF CONTENTS

THE MAP OF THE JEWISH WORLD

It is well-known that R. Zanwill collects stories and legends of the "Jewish Map". That is, of all the places in the world wherein Jews have lived, moved and had their being. Important as is the historical aspect of the life they led, he is more deeply interested in the legendary part of their existence. The historical record, he maintains is a thing of the past, having had a transitory and ephemeral existence. On the other hand, the legends clinging to their history are more abiding, less fleeting than the factual events. For this reason, has he already collected and published thousands of these tales, embracing Jewish life and vicissitudes both in Israel and in the Golah legends which embrace pain and suffering, vision and reality. Reb Zanwill, on one occasion, asked one of his disciples to outline and sketch a Jewish map of the world which should delineate all those places which had some connection with Jewish life. His disciple did so and asked his master to indicate prominently all those places with which Jewish life was linked. Thanking his disciple for the conscientious labour the drawing of such a universal map entailed, he told his devoted disciple that this map was not the one he had in mind, good though it was in its own way. What he really had in mind was a map which would prominently feature all the countries and places to which colourful features of Jewish belief and legend clung and adorned.

Reb Zanwill was asked: "Is the map of the Jewish world different from that of the general world? Is it so different from the one I have sketched?" The retort was: "A thousand times 'Yes'. Not only is the Jewish map greater in length and width, it is also larger in every other dimension." His disciple remained unconvinced. "But, how is this possible? he queried. Reb Zanwill replied: "On the Jewish map of the world which I envisaged, there are centres of Jewish life and visions, centres which are not at all indicated in the Atlas of the world." "What exactly do you mean by this?", he was again asked. Again came the reply of his leader: "I will endeavour to explain this to you."

The Jewish map should feature Paradise (Gan Eden) which exists somewhere in the universe. But does mankind know exactly where it is situated? Again: the Jewish map should locate a place called Luz in which its dwellers know no death. But who can identify it? Where is the "Heavenly Jerusalem' which spans earth and sky and which takes pride of place in the soul of our people? Can you place it exactly on the map of the world? And where will you locate on the map the river Sambatyon which rests on the Shabbat? And where will you place Zebul, where Messiah patiently waits until he receives the Divine bidding to usher in the Messianic Age?"

Reb Zanwill went on: "And where, pray tell me, will you place the land of the "Bnei Msheh", around which there cluster legions of wondrous tales and which occupies a prominent niche in the Jewish world? Where, also, are the mysterious countries occupied by the Ten Tribes, such as Gozan, Habor, Ginzak—and other such fabulous places prominently featured in our legends? Moreover, where are the Kingdoms of Havillah, mentioned by David Ha're'ubeni, the messenger sent to Eretz Israel by the tribe of Reuben? Do you know anyone who can put his finger *exactly* on the spot of the global map where the "Mountains of Darkness" are situated, as well as where are the legendary *Tehom* and the *Sh'eol Tahtit,* the "nether regions" which house Hades and the graves below?"

Reb Zanwill concluded by pointing out to his disciples the names of scores of other places that had left their impress on Jewish

life and thought throughout the winding procession of the centu-
ries. On account of their fabulous importance, he urged his disciple
to try again and sketch a new Jewish map of the world.

Those who move in the circle of Reb Zanwill and who drink
with thirst the endless tales of wonder which cascade from the
perennial fountain of his fertile imagination, are of the opinion that
it will take many, many years before such a map as the one he
envisages can be sketched—if ever at all. Why? Because such a
map would be as endless as is the destined tale of the Jewish nation,
assured as it is, both in history and in legend, to outlive Time and
to exhaust Eternity itself.

*In the beginning of our trip to the triangle of Tiberias, Meron
and Tsafath we stopped by at the cave of the ordination.*

Rabbi Yehuda ben Baba

THE CAVE OF ORDINATION

Towards the end of the ZEBULUN Valley and the border of the Lower Galilee mountains, not far from SHAFRA'AM, on the side of the path leading down to USHA—one of the Ten Seats of the SANHEDRIN—there is a Cave which tradition connects with Rabbi Yehuda ben Baba. By those who lived nearby, it is called "The CAVE OF THE DAUGHTERS OF JACOB", in honour of the pious women who frequently visit the Cave, in order to white-wash the tombstone and to kindle oil-lamps nearby.

Near the Cave is the "Jewish Brook" (WADI AL-YAHUD). In this WADI, the pious immerse themselves prior to entering the Cave. Later generations have renamed it "THE CAVE OF ORDI-NATION". The Rabbi of the Old City of Jerusalem followed a very interesting custom. Whenever a student of the Yeshivah was about to be ordained by him as Rabbi (SEMICHA), he would dispatch him first to the Cave of R. JUDAH b. BABA, so that he could be united in spirit with the memory of this great ZADIK who made every strenuous effort to preserve the chain of traditional SEMICHA of the Rabbis throughout the eventful and winding procession of the generations.

It once happened that the Roman emperor—the ruler of the Holy Land—issued a decree that any Rabbi who ordains a disciple and confers upon him the title of HACHAM (Sage or Rabbi) will deserve the penalty of death. Moreover, death will also be meted out to the newly-ordained Rabbi, the city in which this ordination took place will be destroyed, and the adjacent places will also be uprooted.

So what did R. JUDAH ben BABA do? He made his seat between two great mountains and between two great cities and two Shabbat boundaries; namely, between SHAFRA'AM and USHA, and there ordained five Elders. When the Roman enemy learnt of what had happened, R. Judah b. Baba advised the five new Sages to flee from there. When they asked their Teacher: "And what will happen to you?", his reply was: "I will throw myself down before the enemy like an unwanted stone"; that is, in the hope that they will take no notice of him.

The story (as told in the Talmud, tractate Sanhedrin), concludes thus: "The Romans did not budge from the place (where he was lying huddled in a heap) before they had pierced him with 300 spears of iron, leaving his dead body resembling a sieve on account of the many holes with which it had been dented" . . .

The songs of the Kinereth come from the Well of Miriam from the desert the Midbar.

Rabbi Zanwill

THE WELL OF MIRIAM

When the Israelites wandered in the wilderness, they drank of the water known as the "Well of Miriam", in the belief that it was due to her righteous mode of living that God had created this source of living water. It accompanied our ancestors throughout their eventful, protracted wanderings on the way to the Promised Land. A unique feature of this well was that its waters began to cascade only through the power of song which the Children of Israel sang as they gathered around it prior to drawing water therefrom. A proof? The Bible records that our ancestors sang as they approached it: "Arise, O Well, answer!" Yes, it was thanks to the singing around it, that its crystal-clear waters began to gush forth therefrom, as if in a responding, silent and harmonious melody.

When the Children of Israel crossed the Jordan and settled in Israel, the Well rolled along with them, but when it came to the Sea of Kinneret and flowed into the Lake of Kinneret, the latter took the shape of a harp and became to be known henceforth by the name of KINNERET (a harp). According to legend, the Well flows therein to this very day. Masters of geography and topography know its exact identification.

Many important, therapeutic values are associated with the waters of the Well. It quenches thirst for a long time, it brings healing to the sick and broadens the mind and the heart towards a better understanding, as well as opening the mouth to utter eloquent speech and majestic song.

Cabbalists are fond of relating concerning two disciples of the *ARI* who could not find expression for their emotions, until the

Master led them to the mouth of the Kinneret and gave them its water to drink.

R. HAYIM VITAL knew the eternal secrets of the Torah, but could not declare them to others prior to his drinking its waters. The heart of R. ISRAEL MINZARA hummed inwardly with paeans of song, but they were all still-born, impotent to emerge from his heart until he had drunk of the waters of the Well. No sooner had he done so, however, than the songs pent up so long within him, simply cascaded forth in mighty torrents.

ZINDI hearkened to every word uttered by Reb Zanwill with open-mouthed interest, though she was unable to understand him entirely, since he intertwined his explanations with rabbinical utterances. But his voice and style of speech held her—and the others—spellbound, as if they had been electrified and mesmerized.

Reb Zanwill continued: "We have a tradition that Miriam's Well is especially active during the WATER-LIBERATION ceremonies during the SUKKOT Festival and displays its powers throughout far-flung places at the termination of the Shabbat. It is at that time that Elijah has frequently appeared before Jewish homes mysteriously, in the guise of a water-carrier, bringing the healing-waters of the Well to the needy and the sick, curing those who were inflicted with eye-troubles and bringing speech to those who were dumb, or otherwise inarticulate in their expression.

The world is a mysterious "Pardes" garden. The one man that entered the garden, walked there and came out safely was Rabbi Akiba. His grave called the "best hotel" is in Tiberias.

The Pardes

THE BEST HOTEL

There are many good hotels in Tiberias to which those sick in spirit and body always flocked to find therein rest and security in the shade of glorious Kinnereth. Yet should a visitor there chance to meet one of the elders there who dabble in mysticism and enquire of him of the whereabouts of "the best hotel," he would smilingly point with his finger to the hill and the Cave to which tradition has assigned to be the sepulchre of R. Akiba.

This cave is "the best hotel" in their eyes and unto it do they repair on nights when rain pours down heavily, in order to seek shelter in the vicinity of this Zaddik and be united with him in the spirit of his teaching. The cave is actually a cave within a cave, the inner one being closed to strangers. It is called "the best hotel," because of a very old story cited in the Midrash.

R. Akiba, the greatest scholar of his age who used to affix little crowns to the letters of the Torah, also associated himself with Bar Cochba's rebellion and stirred on the nation towards making a bid for its redemption from the Roman subjection. For many years, did he sit in prison where he was tortured with combs of iron grated over his naked body.

It once happened that he was languishing in a prison in Caesarea. As a rule, one of his disciples Joshua Ha'gorsi by name, was close by in order to know what they were doing to his beloved Master. One Erev Yom Kippur, he gained permission from his interned teacher to go home. As he was about to enter, Elijah appeared at the door and said: "Joshua, halt!" When Joshua asked: "Who art thou?", the reply he received was: "I am Elijah, the priest, and I have come to inform you that your teacher, R. Akiba has now joined the invisible heavenly choir and that the last words which his lips formed on earth were those of the *Shema*. His *Ehad* is still echoing around the world."

The two of them, Elijah and Joshua, immediately repaired to the prison where they found the gates open and the chief warden, as well as all the prisoners were fast asleep. As for R. Akiba, he was peacefully lying in his bed—dead. Elijah stepped up to the dead Rabbi and placed him on his shoulders. When Joshua saw what was happening, he said: "Rabbi, did you not say that you are a Cohen? And surely you know that a cohen must not come into contact with the dead." Elijah replied: "Joshua, my son, know thou that there is no impurity attached to the righteous even when they are dead."

As they left the prison, they heard many angelic hosts mourning: "The Lord hath done righteously, and His judgments are with Israel." Throughout the night did they march, the path as brightly illumined before them as with the brightness of the firmament. When they reached the place, they ascended three steps and descended three steps and then a very beautiful cave opened before them. On entering, they found a bed all ready made, with a stove, table and Menorah.

Elijah tenderly grasped R. Akiba at the head of his body and Joshua at the feet and laid him ever so gently on the couch. As they did so, the Menorah became alight of its own accord and the table set itself in perfect order. As soon as they left the cave, it became hermetically sealed. They then exclaimed: "Happy art thou, R. Akiba, in having found such a good hotel."

THE GRAVE OF R. AKIBA

R. AKIBA, whose grave is in TIBERIAS, was a shepherd for forty years. For another forty years, he studied Torah assiduously and for the remaining forty years of his life he was a celebrated teacher and leader in Israel. He was at the side of BAR COCHBA in his brave but hopeless insurrection against the mighty and cruel Roman Empire that oppressed Judea over whom she had domain.

R. JUDAH relates: When Moses ascended on High after having left this earthly scene, after a full 120 years of life, he came across the Holy One, blessed be He, busily occupied adorning little crownlets to each letter of the Torah (—according to tradition, these were 600,00 in number, thus equating the number of Israelites who unanimously proclaimed the two Hebrew words NA'ASEH VE-NISHMA (We will fulfill and understand), when they were given the DECALOGUE from SINAI's peak).

Moses, surprised at what he saw, asked the Almighty: "What is the purpose of all these decorative crownlets?" Replied the Almighty: "After many generations have elapsed and have been gathered into the past, a man AKIBA, the son of Joseph by name, will arise and expound over every letter. Its crownlet spells heaps upon heaps of HALACHIC import and significance." R. AKIBA, very impressed, then said: "Lord of the universe! Do, please, show me who this will be." The reply he received was: "Turn your gaze behind you and you will see him."

Moses then sat down in the eighth row behind the teacher R. AKIBA, but he could not grasp what they were discussing at all. He felt very dispirited. Fancy, they were discussing the very Torah he had himself taught Israel and yet it all now seemed to unintelligible to him. His dilemma however, did not persist for long. For when R. AKIBA was trying to explain a *moot* point of the Halacha which his disciples failed to understand, they asked: "Rabbi, whence do you derive this explanation?" Their teacher answered: "Well, this explanation is derived from a ruling given by none other than Moses, our first great Teacher himself when he handed down to Israel the Torah he had learnt on Sinai from God's own lips." When Moses heard this, his mind was appeased and he turned once again to the Almighty with the added question:

"Lord of the universe! Since there is such a great scholar, why did you hand over the Torah to me to give to Israel and not to him?" God replied: "Please, hold your peace. This was my decision—and that is that." Moses continued his argument: "Lord of the world! Do show me what reward he will receive for his teaching." Replied the Almighty: "Turn your gaze behind you and you will see for yourself." Moses did so, and a gasp of pained surprise escaped his lips. For what he saw was his horrible sufferings.

Moses could no longer restrain his pained amazement: "Lord of the universe!", he exclaimed bitterly. "Is this the reward for the Torah he had taught with so much self-sacrifice and physical immolation?" Again came the divine reply: "Hold your peace! This was my decision."

R. AKIBA was employed by KALBA SABVA—one of the richest men in Jerusalem of his day—as a humble shepherd. When the latter's daughter saw how humble yet distinguished Akiba was, she approached him with the question: "Will you repair to the BET—HA'MIDRASH to study if I give you my hand in marriage?" This, Akiba eagerly promised to do, for the love between them was deep and mutual. Both their hearts yearned to be united and to beat as one. A clandestine betrothal between them took place and they both pledged their troth to each other in affection and sincerity, hoping to live one day together as man and wife.

When KALBA SABVA was made aware of what had happened without his knowledge and sanction, he banished his daughter from his home and took a vow that she would not inherit any of his vast possessions at his death. Despite this punishment, his daughter was undeterred and decided to implement their secret betrothal with a public wedding.

During the cold winter months, their bedroom was a haystack. Each morning, the doting husband would pick out the straw which still clung to her hair. So touched was Akiba by his wife's devotion and dedication to his studies, that he one day said to her: "Had I the means, I would present you with a golden brooch on which the word JERUSALEM was inscribed and set in precious gems."

One day, the prophet Elijah, disguised as an ordinary mortal, stood at the entrance of the haystack which was their humble home and begged them to give him a bundle of straw, adding: "My wife has just given birth to a child and I have no bed on which to make her and her newly-born babe comfortable."

AKIBA turned to his wife and said: "You see, my dear, this poor man does not even possess any bundles of straw." Her retort was: "You go now and study in the BET HA'MIDRASH." He complied with her request. For twelve solid years he sat in the BET HA'MIDRASH, studying under the tutorship of the renowned TANNAIM, R. ELIEZER and R. JOSHUA.

When this period had elapsed, he returned home accompanied by 12,000 disciples. Little wonder that everybody turned out to meet him and give him a hearty welcome home. When his wife heard the glorious news, she also wished to join the welcoming throng. When her neighbours heard of her intention, they advised her to borrow a decent dress worthy of such an august occasion. Her reply to them was in the words of the Book of Proverbs: "The righteous knows the desire of his animal." When she came near Akiba, she bowed herself to the ground, as if worshipping the very ground on which he trod. When Akiba observed that his disciples, under the impression that she was a strange woman, sought to thrust her aside, he called out to them: "Let her be; for all that I and you have in the way of learning, is entirely due to her."

When her father heard that a great scholar had come to the city, he also decided to go to him and seek his help in nullifying the harsh vow he had made, for his conscience smote him whenever he beheld to what dire penury his vow had reduced his only daughter. When he came before R. AKIBA—whom he did not recognize as his former shepherd—the Rabbi said to him: "Had you known, at the time of your vow, that her husband would one day become as celebrated a scholar as I am reputed to be, would you still have pronounced on her this rash and cruel vow?" The heart-broken father replied: "I would not have uttered such a vow even if her heart's delight had even known only one chapter of the Bible or one *Halacha* of Judaism." AKIBA then smilingly reassured him that none other than he was the husband of his banished daughter. Kalba Sabva fell to the ground and kissed the feet of his famous son-in-law. The aftermath of this momentous and touching interview was that the penitent father-in-law bestowed half of all his possessions to the couple he had formerly banished from his presence.

R. AKIBA chanced once to be on the road of one of his many journeys. When he came to a certain village, he sought food and lodging for the night at one of the inns there only to be refused for apparently no valid reason whatsoever. Akiba bit his lips and murmured to himself: *"All that the Holy One does is for the best."* Having no other alternative, he passed the night in the field. With him as his travelling companions, were an ass, a cockerel, and a lamp. (The ass on which to travel, the cockerel to awaken him at dawn, and the lamp by which he could study at night.)

During that night, a lion came and devoured the ass; a wild cat came and ate up the cockerel, and to add to the misery, a strong gust of wind rendered the lamp ineffectual. The reaction of R.

Akiba when he opened his eyes the next morning and saw what had befallen him was to utter his favourite maxim! "ALL that the Holy One does is eventually for the best of all concerned."

That very night, when Akiba had incurred these personal losses, a group of armed robbers had raided the village, taking most of its dwellers into captivity with them. When R. Akiba was later told of what had happened, he told those who had come to tell him this news: "Well, did I not tell you before this took place that: "ALL THAT GOD DOES IS ULTIMATELY FOR THE GOOD OF ALL?"

THE SEPULCHRE OF
R. MEIR BA'AL HA'NESS

On the road towards the sea of Tiberias, there is a signpost which directs to the grave of *R. MEIR BA'AL HA'NESS.* It is not known for certain to which R. MEIR this refers; hence a diversity of opinion exists as to his exact identity. Generally speaking, opinion leans toward the belief that he was none other than the TANNA R. MEIR, the disciple of R. AKIBA who was so eager to learn Torah that he was even a follower of Rabbi ELISHA b. ABUYA who, on account of his untraditional tendencies and drift from observances, was called by the Rabbis *AHER,* a word which means "the other one." For so far had he wandered from accepted beliefs, that the Rabbis were disinclined even to mention him by name. In justification of R. MEIR's attitude, the Rabbi's defended him by observing: "R. Meir found a pomegranate: after casting away its outer peel, he ate its contents." In other words, so keen was R. Meir to imbibe the wisdom uttered by AHER, that he was impervious and uninfluenced by his outward manifestations.

The real name of R. MEIR was NEHORAI, a word which also means light, for R. Meir enlightened the eyes of the wise with Torah. His descent was from proselytes who traced their ancestry back to King Nero. Of R. Meir, it was said that God knew that there would be none greater than he in his generation.

On account of oppression, R. Meir was compelled in his old age, to flee to a place called ASIA, where he breathed his last. Prior to his death, he requested that he be buried on the shore of the sea. His coffin was placed in a small boat which the winds carried to TIBERIAS where he had lived and taught. The boat refused to stir further. The people were surprised to behold an empty boat with no captain or sailor therein, standing at the shore of the sea and refusing to budge onwards. This extraordinary phenomenon filled their hearts with great trepidation. Fear gripped all who beheld this extraordinary sight.

Their amazement was increased by leaps and bounds when they suddenly beheld a great light sparkling from the boat. When they approached the boat in order to discover the source of this dazzling effulgence, their eyes were confronted by a most miraculous vision. There was R. Meir lying dead on the deck, bathed in a splendid light. They lost no time in removing his body and buried him on the shore of the sea. Those who promenade on the shore of Lake KINNERET, often behold an extraordinary light flashing from the signpost, indicating the spot where the earthly remains of the great R. MEIR were interred.

HOW R. MEIR BANISHED SATAN

As a general rule, people hesitate in trepidation prior to entering a deserted ruin. This fear is rooted in the terror cast by Satan on mankind. Mystics aver that he lingers and hovers above and about ruins and thick forests. There is, however, in TIBERIAS a very ancient ruin believed to date back to Temple days and into which people are not afraid to enter. Why not? Because since R. Meir banished him from there, Satan has been debarred from entering it again.

In ancient times, this ruin houses two men who had made it their dwelling-place. Throughout the six days of the week, they lived within it in peace, being too much preoccupied with their various occupations to find time for one another. The quarrels between them commenced at the approach of SHABBAT, when they returned home to rest from their hard toil for a day. It was on this day of rest that Satan became their fellow-dweller in this ruin. Naturally, he was invisible to them but there he was, safely ensconced in one of the corners of this ruin *cum* dwelling-place.

As long as Satan dwelt with them, quarrels broke out thick and fast. One of the two had only to do something questionable to the other, when Satan jumped out of his corner and whispered derogatory and cantankerous words into the ears of the other. This, Satan constantly did from one to the other, enticing each in turn to quarrel with the other. Satan was not happy unless he succeeded in flaring up a terrible battle-royal between them accompanied with insults and physical attacks.

It once happened that R. Meir was invited to be their guest—that same R. MEIR whose real name was R. NEHORAI (LIGHT), because not only was he filled with the light of the Torah but also because he possessed the power to see things invisible to others. As his two hosts were talking to him, he could see Satan dancing about from one to another. R. Meir remained with them for three weeks, during which time he nullified the malicious and poisonous whisperings of Satan by his sweet words of reasonableness and consideration. When R. Meir observed that a quarrel was about to break out between them, due to the Satanic machinations, he calmed their fury, with the result that concord and amity dwelt within the two hosts.

After three weeks had elapsed and as the three of them sat talking peacefully and lovingly together, they heard a very loud bang, as if a thunder-clap had burst on the ruin. The door of the cave had closed itself and, from the threshold without, a wailing voice could be heard. It was the voice of Satan who had left, frustrated and in tempestuous fury. As he abandoned the cave, never to return there again, he yelled in a voice of bitterness and sheer defeat: "Woe unto me, for it is R. MEIR who has cast me out of this house."

Satan has never come back again to this deserted ruin near Tiberias.

THE RETURN OF THE PLEDGE

BERURIAH, the wife of R. MEIR, was cradled in piety and learning in the home of her distinguished father R. HANINA b. TRADYON, one of the TEN MARTYRS of the HADRIANIC persecutions (135 C.E.). She was held in the greatest esteem by the Rabbis of her day on account of her great wisdom and scholarship. In the religious disputations which her renowned husband often had with the SADDUCEES, she was of the greatest assistance to him. Indeed, many of these confrontations were crowned with triumph for R. Meir, thanks to the skilful arguments advanced by BERU-RIAH.

Like her saintly father, she was ever ready to forgive even those who plagued them with their *deeds* and *creeds*. It happened once when R. Meir prayed that Heaven punish those who cease-lessly oppressed him, she stopped him doing so by saying: "Does not the Psalmist (CXIX.) say: 'SINS will cease,' not that SINNERS will be exterminated?" When R. Meir heard her utter these words, he was so impressed with her humane feelings which were sur-charged with love towards all and malice towards none, that he kissed her on the head. Calm was restored where indignation had seethed before.

They had two lovely, clever children, renowned for their intel-ligence and comely appearance. All who saw them prophesied, with certainty, that a most brilliant future awaited each of them. Their father took a delight in teaching them Torah, while their mother constantly nurtured them in kindliness and consideration for all those with whom they came into contact. No parent could have bestowed a greater love on their children than did R. MEIR and his wife BERURIAH.

It happened once that R. MEIR was away for many days with some of his rabbinical colleagues in another city, far away from his home. On the day when he plied his way homeward, his two children came back from school and told their mother that they had been feeling unwell for the last few hours. Looking at their flushed faces, their mother became anxious and at once put them to bed. A few hours later, they suffered a stroke and died instantaneously. When Beruriah beheld what had happened, it was as if a thunderbolt had struck the house, shattering all that was near and dear to her. There were her two lovely hostages to fortune, "those two feathers plucked from the pinions of love and dropped into the lap of motherhood," lying devoid of every spark of life.

She was aware that her husband was due back this very day. What could she now do to comfort him? How was it best to break the tragic news gently? She girded herself with lion's-strength and took a sheet and covered up her two dead children. She sat at the bedside, shrouded in silent grief, with a heart almost at breaking-point.

When her husband entered, she received him lovingly with calm in her voice and with a brave demeanor. When he enquired how the children were, she assured him that if he possessed himself with patience, she would soon usher him into their bedroom. After he had rested for a while and taken some light repast, Beruriah said she had first a very important legal question *(DIN TORAH)* for him to answer. When he asked her to tell him what this was, she gave him this reply: "It happened once that a man entrusted into my safe keeping a pledge of two silver cups to look after until he called for their return. As these cups were of the most precious kind, I looked after them as "the apple of my eye." He came today and asked for their immediate return. Now tell me, Meir," she asked with a break in her voice, "Should I have returned them to him or not?"

R. Meir was amazed at his clever wife posing such a simple question to him. Coming from one renowned for her learning and wisdom, he could hardly contain his surprise! "Is this a question," he asked, "to return a pledge or not?" Words began to fail him in his blank amazement. But before he could say more, she took him tenderly by the hand and led him softly into the bedroom where the children lay, locked in the arms of death.

She carefully lifted up the sheet and his eyes beheld his two lovely children, frigid and cold, after having been touched by the finger of the Angel of Death. When R. Meir began to lament bitterly and to bang his head against the wall in tragic reaction at what had happened, his wife softly reminded him of the answer he had just given to her question about immediately returning the pledge which was deposited only for a short time.

"Well," she continued, "our two children, those two lovely flowers which bloomed in our home till today, were the pledges given to us by God. 'He hath given, and He hath now taken away; may His Name be blessed.'" When R. Meir heard this, he accepted the Divine decree with resignation. Turning to his wife, he said: "You are true to your name BERURIAH. You are clear in your comfort, and blessed will you be forever."

A GIFT FOR THE MESSIAH

Special care is bestowed by Reb Zanwill as Director of Religious places in Israel on the traditional tomb of Maimonides in Tiberias. Not only did he devote an entire book to his life and work and takes part in the study circles that pore over the works of the Master, but he also arranged for a garden to be planted around the tomb to which pilgrimage takes place on Tebet 20th, the anniversary of his death (1204).

On each Yahrzeit, the Director leads a party to the grave where they spend time studying sections of his encyclopedic work. This is a pilgrimage with a difference. Unlike pilgrimages to other graves, at which candles are kindled, Memorial prayers recited and petitions received, it was felt that such practices would be frowned upon by one who was a rational philosopher and spurned anything of a superstitious nature. Hence the pilgrimage has not caught the fire of the masses who prefer emotional ceremonies but is beloved by the intellectual.

In fact, the Director was once questioned by a scholarly Rabbi why he had organized such a pilgrimage, knowing only too well that this was against the grain of the philosophy of Maimonides. In the course of the discussion between them, the Director had no difficulty in convincing the Rabbi that despite his philosophic tendencies, Maimonidies also possessed mystical propensities. To prove this, he narrated to the Rabbi the legend which tells how the Master came to be buried in Tiberias.

Maimonides had lived many years in Egypt (Fostat, now Cairo), where he was the royal physician. Despite the occasional tongue of anti-semitism, he was beloved by the general populace. The tongue of slander was silenced against him and he remained the trusted doctor of royalty and the respected teacher of all. But though he lived in Egypt, his heart was always in Israel; and in the Will he drew up, he entreated his disciples to bring his earthly remains to Eretz Israel.

This wish was granted. A few years after his passing, his coffin was placed on a camel and proceeded to the Holy Land. It was then that strife broke out between the other Holy Cities, all of which wanted the Master to be buried in its soil. The main contenders to this honour were Jerusalem, Hebron, Zepphat, Safet and Miron, among others. Each one brought most decisive arguments why the privilege should be theirs. To solve the dilemma, it was decided to leave it to the camel that carried the coffin to decide the burial place. The camel then proceeded on its journey and brought this coffin direct to Meron, to the grave of R. Johanan B. Zakkai, of Yavneh fame. Since the camel refused to proceed further, it was decided that Heaven had ordained this to be the burial place.

Why was Tiberias so ordained? Because Maimonides had all his life yearned for Eretz Israel. In fact, alone of all Codists, he dealt and expounded such *halachot* which are relevant only to a life in the Holy Land, the others including in their Codes only such laws which operate in the Golah. Maimonides waited for the coming of the Messiah every moment of his life. In his monumental works, he prepared the Jew for his coming by teaching the laws which will be necessary for all to observe when the Heavenly Kingdom coalesces with life on earth. Hence it was he who formulated in his Thirteen Creeds, the last of which tells the Jew to believe "in perfect faith" that the Messiah, though he tarries, will come one day. It is worthy to remember that with this firm belief, our millions of martyrs marched to their untimely, tortured death in the Nazi concentration chambers.

This firm belief in the coming of the Messiah and his monumental *Mishne Torah* (or *Yad Ha'Hazakah*)—the compendium of Halacha—are in the nature of a gift to the Messiah. So that when he comes, the people will know how to live according to Jewish folkways. Alas, Maimonides did not live to witness the Messianic Age but he died with the gift to the Messiah in his hands. Tiberias was chosen because, like R. Johanan B. Zakkhai, Maimonides believed that the Messiah would first appear there. To this day, the *Yad Ha'hazakah,* does not depart from the study of the Rabbi because, in its pages, are found the maps and detailed routes to be taken by a Jewish State, in which sovereignty and Holiness are wedded.

IT IS ENOUGH IF I AM WITH HIM

On the fourteenth of Iyar, which is the second Passover, many people used to *descend* to Tiberias to celebrate the feast of Rabbi Meir *Bal Hanes* and to visit the tombs of the pious which are in the city and to the tomb of the Rambam, as it was the custom of the elders to do. Many people came a few days earlier, so that they would have time to visit all the tombs.

The curator considered himself to be one of the disciples of the Rambam. Faithful to his will, he locked the tomb of the Rambam on the tenth of Iyar so that no one could visit it. When the pious men arrived at the tomb and found it closed, they were very surprised and they asked the guards the reason why the tomb was closed on that day. The guards replied that it was not their fault, they had done it by order of the curator. The men grumbled and there were even some among them who wanted to break into the tomb by force. They refrained from doing so, however, out of respect for the curator. Instead, they went to him to inquire about it.

When they came to the curator, he understood the reason of their visit and wished to appease them. He invited them to sit down, welcomed them with biblical greetings and offered them fruit. They refused, however, to be bribed into agreement with his action. They asked angrily how could he do such a thing as to prevent Jews from visiting the tomb of the *Rambam?* The curator answered that, by so doing, he was fulfilling the will of the Rambam. The men were astonished to hear these words and asked for further explanation. Those who had previously met with the curator were used to receiving surprising answers, never doubting them. This time, however, they were not satisfied with the answer and demanded that he tell them his real reasons for the deed. Whereupon, the curator took out the Rambam's explanation for the New Year and read to them some passages from it.

"One Saturday night, on the fourth of Iyar, I went to sea. On Friday, the tenth of Iyar, a great storm at sea almost sank us. The sea was very rough and I made a vow . . . that these two days (the day I boarded and the day of the storm) would be fast days for me and all my household and all those attached to me and I will order my children to do so till the end of the generations and also they that give charity according to their means. I vowed that I would sit alone on the tenth of Iyar (the day of the storm). I would not see anyone but would pray and spend the whole day alone, (in memory of) the day I found no one in the sea except G-d! Hence I will not see and sit with anyone except when forced to do so."

On that day, continued the curator, the Rambam was alone with G-d and it is his will always to be so till the end of the generations, namely to be alone with G-d and not to see anyone except Him alone. This he commanded his sons and disciples till the end of Time. Who are we to disturb the Rambam in his isolation with G-d? Who are we to force him to be with others?

The Curator's words so shocked the people that they did not know what to say. Almost all agreed with him, save one old man among them. He turned to the curator: "Curator: it is my considered view that you cannot change the custom of this place, but may keep it open, as it was before. Should you ask: 'Why?' My answer will be that it is because no one among us thinks that when we come to the tomb of the Rambam he comes out to be with us. Nothing of the sort. *He is not with* us, but it is we that are with him. So, please do not interfere with our established custom."

Reb Zanwill didn't agree to him. "The Rambam is with us also," he told him. Nevertheless he opened the gates of the grave.

THE RAMBAM AS A CHILD

The people attached healing powers to the grave of the Rambam (our teacher Moses ben Maimon) and they behaved towards it as towards a righteous man who had the power to save "in the manner that the righteous man declared and the Lord fulfilled his declaration." They behaved towards it, as towards a holy doctor, who even after his death, still served as a faithful doctor helping the sick, aiding the poor and all those struck down by fate. Many parents used to bring their idiot or lazy sons to the grave of the great teacher, so that he could open their hearts and teach them Torah. They believed that the great teacher, the "Guide of the Perplexed," the blind and the stubborn, would be a teacher also to those confused in heart and those lacking in desire.

Rabbi Zanwill tried to reduce this belief in healing powers, but he seemed only to increase the number of the confused and those lacking in desire. Sometimes, he even joined them to tell them a folk-tale regarding the childhood of the Rambam, a tale that had no historical basis but was, nonetheless, beloved by the people.

The child Moses, says the legend, was slow in learning and understanding and excelled in no form. He did not want to learn; whatever he did learn, he did not absorb or remember. The people behaved towards him as towards a confused child and even nicknamed him "son of the butcher."

Rabbi Maimon was sorry about his son who had caused him such shame and embarrassment. Even more sorry was his son, Moses, because of the annoyance and contempt for him that he felt around him. One day, the child Moses fled from the house and found himself a hiding-place in one of the wayfarer's inns that were in the cities of Spain, filled with beggars and transgressors. There he lived their life until he recognized their full ugliness and became disgusted. It was his sorrow that awakened his dormant strength and he was encouraged to mend his ways. He then went to Alisona where stood the famous academy of Rabbi Joseph Hale vi Ibn Migash, and there he learned, diligently. Rabbi Joseph Halevi did not know who the boy was and took him home thinking he was an orphan.

Rabbi Maimon did not know that his son Moses was learning Torah in an academy; when he discovered it by accident several years later, Moses was already a Gaon in Israel who aroused universal wonder and honour.

Rabbi Zanwill cherishes this story and tells it often, even though he knows that the facts are not correct. "The facts are not correct," says the curator, "but the idea is true; every boy, whosoever he may be, and wherever he may live, can raise in himself hidden strength and reach the point of our teacher Moses ben Maimon."

MEKOMOTH KEDOSHIM IN MERON

(3,2) Grave of the Tanai, RABBI SIMON BAR YOHAI, pupil of Rabbi Akiba and author of the Zohar, of whom it was said: "Hail the eye that has seen him." *Grave of his son, RABBI ELEAZAR, Tanai, who used to say: "Whosoever fulfills one single commandment, hail him, for he has brought about the acquittal of himself and of the whole world." In the yard outside the cave is the grave of *RABBI YIBA SABA, at the northern end those of RABBI YOSI BEN KISMA, RABBI TARFON and RABBI BENJAMIN BEN YEFET. *Grave of RABBI YOHANAN THE COBBLER, pupil of Rabbi Akiba, who used to say: "Any assembly which exists for the sake of heaven will endure, any which exists for other ends will not endure." (Avot, 4,11). On Lag Ba'omer s special fire, named after him, it lit on his grave. *(3,3) Cave of the House of Hillel: Grave of HILLEL THE ELDER and many of his pupils. Hillel the Elder was President of the Sanhedrin towards the end of the Second Temple. He used to say: "Be a disciple of Aaron: Love peace and seek peace, love mankind and bring them nearer to the Torah". He also used to say: "If I help not myself, who will help me? And if myself alone, what am I? And if not now, when? * (3,4) Grave of SHAMMAI THE ELDER, Chief Justice in Hillel's time. He used to say: "Study regularly, say little and do much, and meet all men with a pleasant expression." Below the grave is a cave with the sepulchral chambers of 14 pupils of Shammai. The traditional days for the pilgrimage to Meron are: Lag Ba'omer (18 Iyar); 7 Adar, the Feast of Moses; and 25 Elul, the Feast of the Tannai Rabbi Eleazar, son of Rabbi Simon Bar Yohai.

On the way from Meron to the North, at the entrance to Gush Halav, lies the *(3,5) SMR. Grave of SHEMAYA and AVTALION, descendants of Sanherib who became converted to Judaism about 40 B.C.A. Shemaya was president of the Sanhedrin, Avtalion Chief Justice. In these offices they succeeded Simon Ben Shetah and Yehuda ben Tabai. Shammai and Hillel were their faithful disciples. Shemaya used to say: "Love labour and hate the rabbinical office." Avtalion used to say: "Wise men, have a care how ye speak."

I. MERON

Meron is in the Upper Galilee and may well be the city of Merom, the conquest of which the Egyptians marked by a picture in the palace of Ramses II in Upper Egypt. This picture depicts a conquered fortress over which is written, in hieroglyphics, the word "Merom." There is an opinion that the spring of water near Meron is the "waters of Merom mentioned in connection with a battle in the days of Joshua. The place was fortified by Josephus during the War against Rome and was called "Merut." After the Destruction, several priestly families settled there; among them was that of Yehoiriv who had served in the Temple. Throughout the ages, Meron remained a centre of study and prayer. Tradition asserts that R. Shimon bar Yohai lived and taught there. There is still a synagogue from Mishnaic times that is reputed to have been built by him. In the Middle Ages, Meron has deemed most sacred because it was believed to be the grave site of holy men. Many made pilgrimages to the Cave of Hillel and Shammai and to the grave of R. Shimon bar Yohai.

Pilgrimages are still made to Meron. Nearly one hundred thousand people come on Lag B'omer. Men, women and children, of all circles and communities, come and Meron unifies them all. The joyous singing of the pilgrims can be heard throughout the Galilee, in its towns and hills and byways. It is also a custom to go to Meron on the anniversary of Moses' death, the seventh of Adar, as well as on the special day of R. Shimon's son, R. Elazar, the twenty-fifth of Elul.

Meron is nestled among lofty mountains and rests in the shadow of two great cities, Safed and Tiberias. Though small in size, it occupies a most important place in our people's spiritual life. It has even been asserted that it is Meron which has exalted the mountains and that its shadow is cast over Safed and Tiberias rather than visa-versa. This is not far wrong. Meron has indeed had an effect on the two cities as it has had over the entire Galilee; it has cast a mystic spell over the Galilean hills and skies.

Meron is the site of a number of historical landmarks. Each of its secret caves, sacred monuments and numerous graves has its own story; there are customs and beliefs associated with every one. Moreover, they are related to various pilgrimages from medieval times and even earlier.

Legend has it that pilgrims would march up the narrow, hilly path to ancient Meron single file, in a long line. This led to an explanation of the phrase in the Rosh Hashanah prayer, *Untaneh Tokef:* "All the inhabitants of the world pass before Him as *bnei meron* (literally: the sons of Meron)." The words *"bnei meron"* were chosen because the path ascending to Meron was so narrow that two people could not walk side by side.

The League for Sacred Sites has drawn up a map designating the sites to which pilgrims go: Cave of Hillel and Shammai; Graves of R. Shimon bar Yohai and his son Elazar; Burial Places of R. Yohanan Hasandler and R. Yitzhak Napha; and the Idra. Other sites were mentioned by medieval travellers. R. Moshe Basulah recorded that he had prayed alongside the graves of R. Tarfon and R. Yosi ben Kisma. R. Simha of Zaloshitz wrote in his travel book that he saw the Chair of Elijah and visited the graves of the mystic Rav Yibah Saba and of R. Yitzhak. Others added: the Cave of the Priests, R. Ada Saba, Rav Hammunah Saba, R. Benyamin bar Yaffeh, R. Yehuda ben Betera and R. Yosi Hatufa.

In his *Book of Travels* of the year 5281, R. Moshe Basulah wrote: "Afterwards, we diverted the path to Meron, making it curve, because many Jews were walking on the graves of the saints. On Monday, the twenty-fourth of Nisan, I returned to Meron with ten others who made it a practice to go monthly to pray at the grave of R. Shimon bar Yohai. I also prayed then at the graveside of R. Tarfon and of R. Yosi ben Kisma; their graves are at the foot of the mount, in a field opposite the entrance to the synagogue on top. Over both are piles of stones as memorials and a large almond tree grows out of the one over R. Yosi's grave. The burial site of R. Yohanan Hasandlar is near the village, not far from the tanners' cave."

Description of the graves in Meron in the travel account of R. Simha of Zaloshitz:

"Meron is about a half-*parsah* or a little more from Safed [note: a *parsah* is 4.5 kilometers]. We walked there on a Sunday and stayed four days; we visited the grave of R. Shimon bar Yohai.

I am really unworthy to have had the privilege of entering the courtyard of that miracle-worker, R. Shimon bar Yohai, his son, and R. Yitzhak whom the Zohar *(Vayehi)* tells that R. Shimon saved from death. In front of the building was a walled yard; within it, to the right and to the left, were stone-pillars and beamed corridors. A wide wooden door is in the gate; outside it, to the left, is a *tel* (a small hill). That is the grave of Rav Yiba Saba who is mentioned in the Zohar *(Mishpatim)*. We sat down there and studied the passage. To the right of the gate, is the grave of R. Yitzhak; over it, is a structure and, when one comes to Meron, one kindles oil there.

The building itself is quite elegant. It is covered by a large dome and there are cupolas over the graves of R. Shimon and R.

Elazar. Near that of R. Shimon's, is a pillar on which is a vessel containing oil and bits of cotton or flax. When that is lit, light is spread over a considerable distance.

We went to the grave of R. Yohanan Hasandlar; it has a partial stone fence about it. He is buried in a cave over which stands an old wall. People are afraid to enter because a snake is reputed to be there. In front, is a plastered wall with a small, narrow opening. I entered with difficulty and someone said: "Come and I will show you his tannery."; but I did not have time because the group did not want to wait.

On the second day, we walked over the stones of the mountain to the Cave of Hillel. It is a large cave carved out of one stone. In front of the caves, I saw coffins on the ground and their coverings. ——In the northeast corner was the grave of Hillel the Elder, peace be to him . . . We went up the opposite hill and there, in the middle, were the graves of the disciples of Shammai the Elder; they were in low niches in caves. We entered and studied there a while. From there, we proceeded to the top of the mount, to the plain which the Arabs call "Shammai's Field." There are ruins there and it is obvious that there once was a city. That is where the coffins of Shammai and his wife, peace unto them, are.

R. Shmuel from Harobeshob said to me: 'What do you see on the top of the mount?' I replied that I could not see far; I could only see what was near. However, I was able to make out a stone-monument at the top of the opposite hill. He then said: 'That stone is connected to and projects from the mountain. It is a huge stone and there is a tradition that it is called "Elijah's Chair." I wanted to climb up there to see it closely, but it would have taken a day to go there and return."

II. SPECIAL SITES

CAVES of HILLEL and SHAMMAI

Hillel and Shammai were among the greatest men of Jewish history. Tradition tells us that they inherited their leadership positions from Shamayah and Avtalyon and established the two schools, the House of Hillel and the House of Shammai. Both appear in Talmudic literature, in the Mishna , and Tosefta and Beraita, Hillel being portrayed as lenient and Shammai as strict. Hillel became the Patriarch two thousand years ago, a century before the Destruction of the Temple, at the end of the Second Commonwealth era. He was known as "Hillel the Babylonian" and was also called "Disciple of Ezra" because, like Ezra, he came from Babylonia at a time when the Torah was neglected and he fortified it anew. Hillel was a woodcutter who did not permit his poverty to interfere with his study of Torah. He is regarded as a second Moses and it is said that he too lived one hundred and twenty years. He was forty when he came from Babylonia; he spent forty years in studying and was the spiritual leader of the Jewish people for forty years.

Among Hillel's famous dictums are these:

"Be of the disciples of Aaron, loving peace and pursuing peace; loving people and bringing them close to the Torah."

"If I am not for myself, who am I? But if I am only for myself, what am I? If not now, when?"

Shammai the Elder shared Hillel's responsibilities. He used to say: "Set a fixed time for studying the Torah. Say little and do much, and receive every man graciously."

Tradition has it that both men and their disciples were buried near each other. The Cave of Hillel has always been regarded as being on the slope of the mountain. It is large and roomy with many chambers; the burial sites of Shammai and his disciples are nearby. R. Benjamin of Tudela mentions the tradition of the cave containing the graves of Hillel and Shammai and twenty of their disciples; so do others.

There is a unique feature of the Cave of Hillel as that was first mentioned by R. Petahiah of Regensburg: "There is a cave in the Lower Galilee which is wide and high. To the one side is the cave of Shammai and his disciples; to the other, that of Hillel and his. In the middle, there is a huge basin carved like a cup and it can hold more than forty seahs [note: one seah equals 133 litres]. Good people who enter see it full of water. They should wash their hands, pray and request what they will. Those who are not decent cannot see the water. But, if a thousand pitchers of water were drawn from the basin, it would still remain full." R. Shmuel ben R. Shimshon also mentioned this remarkable feature.

"We found in Meron, at the bottom of the mountain, the graves of Hillel and Shammai and 36 other graves. Above them, is a dome of a sort of domestic marble shaped like trees with six basins. We prayed there and we found, to the right, one of the basins full of water. The second was waterless, but the third was also full. On the left, one was half-full and the other was completely full of water. In each corridor are three graves and above, on one side of the graves near the basins, one was full of water and the other empty. The Head of the Exile ordered a wax candle to be lit and to see whence the water entered the basins, but we found nothing. We poured a lot of water to the ground but the basins were not at all diminished. The water was sweet as honey and this was a miraculous thing. Outside the cave entrance, was a large hall with three coffins alongside one another, one being elevated above the others."

THE MEMORIAL of R. SHIMON bar YOHAI and his son, R. ELAZAR

Tradition has marked the graves of R. Shimon and R. Elazar in Meron in a large building with many cupolas overlooking a magnificent mountainous area. R. Shimon bar Yohai was one of the outstanding disciples of R. Akiba and was ordained by him. He is considered the foremost mystic. It is related that he studied Torah with Elijah the Prophet. R. Shimon bar Yohai is cited in the Talmud hundreds of times and he is called simply "R. Shimon." He is the author of the *Sifri*. He was a fearless fighter for his people and completely at home in the world of miracles. It seems that he took part in the undertakings of Bar Kochba and R. Akiba; he wandered through the Galilean towns teaching Torah, love of the land and loyalty. One of his well-known statements is: "The Holy One bestowed three gifts on Israel, but all were acquired only through suffering."

One of them was the Land of Israel.

R. Shimon saw the settlements of Galilee in their decline, people on the move as a result of the Roman persecutions. He urged them to remain in their homes despite the decrees and the hardships. He hated the Romans and spoke harshly about them. He was forced to flee and hide in a cave with his son, Elazar, for thirteen years. Tradition tells that he composed the Zohar, the Book of Books of the mystics, during his stay there.

R. Shimon bar Yohai is highly venerated by the people and there are many legends associated with him. The Zohar, which is attributed to him, became a basic work alongside the Bible, the Talmud and the *Midrashim*. His resting-place, Meron, became one of the sacred sites to which pilgrimages are made.

R. Shimon is regarded as the one who purified the Galilee. Legend has it that the district was very un-Jewish until he established twenty-six synagogues there. The numerical value of twenty-six corresponds to the numerical value of the word indicating God's Being *(Havayah)*. Thus, it was said that he caused God to dwell in the Galilee. He was helped from on high and a great light went forth from the cave in Peki'in and from Meron, causing the Galilee to become a land of mystery and of grace.

R. Elazar son of R. SHIMON

The grave of R. Elazar is alongside that of his father's. He too was a great teacher and mystic. He hid with his father in a cave for thirteen years to escape the Romans who were looking for them. His father esteemed him highly and once said: "I have seen only a few among the initiated and, if there are only two, they are my son and I. Together, we could free the entire world from judgment. *(Succah* 45b)."

The marker on his grave is elongated and surrounded by an iron fence.

Legend relates that R. Elazar was confined for several years in the attic of his home in the village of Gush Halav, near Meron. According to another version, it was in the village of Akhbara. The sages wanted to bury him near his father, but the people of Akhbara did not allow them to remove the body; but once, just before Yom Kippur, when the people of Akhbara were very busy, the men of Biri came and took R. Elazar to the grave of his father in Meron. This legend is repeated in various versions. One has it that R. Shimon bar Yohai appeared to the sages in a dream and said: "I have only one dove in your midst and you do not want to bring it near me." The sages thereupon went to do so. The people of Akhbara, however, did not permit them to do so because all the time that R. Elazar son of R. Shimon remained in his attic, no wild beast ever came to the town. One day, *Erev* Yom Kippur, they were busy and the sages sent the men of Biri who lifted his bier and took it to the cave of his father.

R. YOHANAN HASANDLAR

According to tradition, R. Yohanan Hasandlar, one of the disciples of R. Akiba, was buried in Meron. He used to say: "Every assembly which is in the name of Heaven will in the end be established, but that which is not in the name of Heaven will not in the end be established." (*Avot* IV:14). Every Lag B'Omer, a special flare is kindled at his grave and is designated by his name.

R. Moshe of Basula tells that, in 5185: "In Meron, we went to the grave of R. Yohanan Hasandlar. The yard around it is surrounded by a half-ruined stone fence. He is buried in a cave over which stands an old wall. It is said that a snake lies there and people are afraid to go in." Alongside the grave, carved out of rock, is a small cave. People say that R. Yohanan Hasandlar would there prepare the leather for the shoes he made in order to earn his bread.

The following anecdote reflects the great love of R. Yohanan for the Land of Israel. There is a story that R. Elazar ben Shamua and r. Yohanan Hasandlar used to go to Netzivim (in Babylonia) to study Torah with R. Yehudah b. Betira. When they arrived in Sidon, they remembered *Eretz Yisrael* and began to weep while quoting the verse: "You shall inherit it and dwell therein" (Deut. XI:31). They thereupon returned home and said: "Dwelling in *Eretz Yisrael* outweighs all the other Commandments."

R. YITZHAK NAPHA

R. Yitzhak Napha, one of the foremost Palestinian *amoraim,* is well-known in Talmudic literature. He lived most of his life in Tiberias. The adjective "Napha" (literally, "the smith") indicates his occupation. Two of his noted statements are: "Should one boast that I never exerted myself, yet I found, —do not believe him; but should he answer I exerted myself and I found, then do believe him." (Megillah 6); "One regime comes and another regime goes, but Israel remains forever" *(Kohelet Rabbah)*.

R. Moshe Yerushalmi, who described the graves of Meron in 5129, mentioned R. Yitzhak. In Meron, near the gate to the Courtyard, "somewhat off to the side, is buried the servant of R. Shimon ben Yohai and his name is R. Yitzhak. Over his grave, too, is a monument and it is possible to kindle olive-oil there."

R. YOSI ben KISMA

R. Yosi ben Kisma was a contemporary of R. Akiba. He is depicted in talmudic and *midrashic* literature as a seer who could foretell events and who would give a sign as proof of his predictions. The disciples of R. Yosi ben Kisma once asked him: "When is the Son of David coming?" He replied: "I fear lest you ask me for a sign." They said to him: "We do not make such a request." He answered: "This gate will fall, will be rebuilt and will fall again—and there will not be time to build it again before the Son of David will come." They said: "Master, give us a sign!" He replied: "Did I not tell you that you would demand a sign from me?" They said: "Nevertheless!" He said to them: "The waters of the Cave of Pamyas will turn to blood"—and the waters did so.

RAV HAMNUNA SABA

Tradition places the grave of Rav Hamnuna Saba on the road to Acre, in the neighbourhood of the channel of Brook Meron, alongside the bubbling spring. He is one of the mystics mentioned often in the Zohar. Rahamim Oplatka, in his Travelbook which appeared in 5236, said, in speaking about Meron: "Below is the Cave of Hillel and his disciples and R. Hamnuna Saba."

RAV YIBA SABA

Among the graves discovered by R. Isaac Luria was that of
Rav Yiba Saba, mentioned in the Zohar as one of the mystics. It is
told that he had but to cast a look at a person to change him into a
pile of bones. R. Haim Vital reported that R. Isaac Luria came
across Rav Yiba's grave in the vicinity of Safed, alongside a well
called in Arabic *"Bir Alsheikh"* (The Sheik's Well). It is off the
road to Meron. At the top of the mountain, on somewhat level
ground, there is a boulder and, near it, is the grave of Rav Yiba
Saba.

Another well-known tradition puts his grave in Meron, near
that of R. Shimon bar Yohai, in the cave in front of the gate to the
courtyard, to the right.

R. BINYAMIN

R. Binyamin bar Yaffet was a Palestinian *amora* of the third
generation. He was a disciple of R. Yohanan and of R. Elazar and
he transmitted a number of legends in their name. Tradition places
his grave in Meron.

THE IDRA [note: It is also the name of one of the books of the Zohar]

The site of the Idra is found on the road from Safed to Meron.
The Ministry of Religions has repaired the Cave of the Idra which
had actually been discovered by R. Isaac Luria. It is told in the
Shaar Hagilgulim, that Luria would take his followers to the village
of Meron where R. Shimon bar Yohai used to gather his disciples
in order to initiate them into the Great Idra. Luria would say: "R.
Elazar would sit here, and R. Aba there," and so name them all.
He would seat each of his disciples in the place appropriate for

him, in accordance with his soul. He would say that each one had a spark of one of R. Shimon's group and would reveal to them deep mysteries. He would say: "If only you would be able to see, you would see a large group of saints and angels who came to listen to the Idra and a crackling fire all about."

THE CAVE of the PRIESTS

At the top of the hill rising to the South, is the cave which Jews call "The Cave of the Priests." It seems that the priests of ancient Meron were interred here. The disciple of R. Haim b. Atar tells of his visit with his master to Meron in 5102: "Nearby is a big cave called 'the Cave of the Priests.'" It was said that a woman once came there with her son. He entered the cave alone and when they looked for him and found him in the cave, he said: "Several men dressed in white are here and they kissed me and blessed me."

ELIJAH'S CHAIR

On top of the highest mount stands a boulder overlooking the expanse. That is the site of the rock called "the Chair of Elijah," Elijah being the prophet who is to bring the message of redemption and announce the Messiah who, according to tradition, will appear in the Galilee. Many stories and legends are told about Elijah, his house in Tsafath and chair in Meron.

III. PILGRIMAGES TO MERON

Meron is one of the oldest sites to which Jews made pilgrimages. This is indicated even in the earliest literature. Medieval travellers mentioned that people would go to pray at the water-pool there. The special day for pilgrimages was the fourteenth of Adar *(Pesah Sheini)*. People would make their way to the Cave of Hillel and Shammai, because the miracle of water was widely known. The author of TOTZAOT ERETZ YISRAEL referred to this practice and wrote: "The Cave of Shammai and Hillel, and their thirty-two disciples, is in Meron. Jews and Arabs gather there on *Pesah Sheini* and the Jews pray and recite psalms. When they see water coming into the cave, they rejoice because it is a sign that the year has been blessed. Often, there was no water at all but, while they prayed, it suddenly appeared."

The Unknown people from Kandish, who mentioned special pilgrimages to the grave of R. Shimon, connected them with the Cave of Hillel and the blessings of water: "There is a cave in Meron where the important elders are buried, among them Shammai and Hillel. A little farther on, there is another cave in which R. Shimon ben Yohai and his son are buried, and there is the synagogue of R. Shimon. As there is no fresh water there, people cannot live there; but Jews come on the Three Festivals to visit the graves of the aforementioned saints, particularly that of R. Shimon ben Yohai. They pray to God that He should give them water and they remain there for several days; then rain comes down at once. The Arabs fill their wells and their vessels and then they give the Jews good things to eat and drink."

R. Yitzhak Latif relates something similar in his epistle. During a drought, men and women went to pray in the Cave and God hearkened to their prayers. First, the border-stones of the cave became full, then the clouds gathered, rain descended, and they drank. R. Joseph Karo tells in his *Maggid Mesharim:* "Know this: whenever rain is greatly needed, go to the graves of these saints and you will be answered."

From the time of R. Isaac Luria onwards, when as the Zohar and Kabbala spread throughout Galilee, people would go to the grave of R. Shimon bar Yohai to learn mystical secrets. The author of *Shivhei Ha-ari* regards such a pilgrimage as an absolute requirement for initiates into mysticism.

People would remain there for ten days to study the Zohar. The Galilean mystics revived the celebration of R. Shimon bar Yohai in Meron on Lag B'omer, kindling a special flame at his grave and studying Zohar passages. According to their tradition, the book was concealed in Meron until an Arab found it and handed it over to merchants in the Upper Galilee.

This was the time when the date of the pilgrimage was moved from *Pesah Sheini* to Lag B'omer, or rather it began on *Pesah Sheini,* continued for three or four days and concluded at the grave of R. Shimon bar Yohai on Lag B'omer. That day then took on a festive character everywhere, particularly in Meron.

R. Moshe Bascula reports: "On the fourteenth of Iyar, which is called *Pesah Sheini,* a large caravan arrived at Meron. There were more than a thousand people, many having come from Damascus with their wives and children and many from Safed. All went to Peki'in, the village of the cave in which R. Shimon bar Yohai and his son hid for thirteen years. The well is still there but the carob tree is gone. People also came to Meron from all around and remained two complete days celebrating and rejoicing. We prayed at the graves of all the holy men there."

Lag B'omer is accepted as a festive break in the *sefirah* mourning period, during which there are no festivities, or weddings or haircuts. Lag B'omer is a break in the sadness and is considered a minor festival on which weddings are held, haircuts allowed and when people go to the fields with bows and arrows. Pilgrimages are made to the graves of holy men, especially at Meron.

It is difficult to ascertain the exact origin of Lag B'omer, particularly of the Celebration of R. Shimon bar Yohai. Several reasons are given for the festive nature of the day. In general, it is considered an expression of gratitude for the cessation of the plague that had spread among the disciples of R. Akiba, as related in the Talmud *(Yevamot 62b):*

"R. Akiba had twelve thousand pairs of students and all died at one time between Pesah and Shavuot, because they did not respect one another. The world was being destroyed until R. Akiba went to the sages in the South and taught R. Meir, R. Yehuda, R. Yosi, R. Shimon (bar Yohai) and R. Elazar ben Shammua. He told them: 'The others died only because they begrudged each other their knowledge of Torah. Take heed that you be not like them.' They arose and filled all of *Eretz Yisrael* with Torah." The Gaonic tradition is that the plague ceased on Lag B'Omer.

Some people connect the plague with the Bar Kochba rebellion which, according to Josephus, began on Lag B'Omer and in which R. Akiba and his disciples took an active part. Lag B'Omer is also associated with R. Shimon bar Yohai who was born and who died in that day and was buried in Meron.

The Kindling

According to the mystics, the kindling of fire is a symbol of the Zohar which revealed the hidden light which spread throughout the world from the pillar of fire which appeared to R. Shimon bar Yohai and his colleagues. This pillar of fire continues to burn and to lift man's inner spirit up to the Upper Light, to the Divine Revelations which flow through the flame to the infinite. On Lag B'Omer, the day of R. Shimon bar Yohai's departure from the world, he elevated the Upper Light to unveil many secrets which still hover about and are revealed in the burning fire.

Others regard the kindling of fire as a symbol of the fire which surrounded R. Shimon bar Yohai's home, body and coffin on the day of his death, as it is related in the Zohar. The mystics begin their Lag B'Omer vigil in Meron with this tale:

It has been taught that on the day that R. Shimon was to depart from this world and was arranging his affairs, the disciples entered his house. R. Elazar his son, and R. Aba and others stood before him. R. Shimon lifted his eyes and saw that the house was full. . . . Before they sat down, he opened his eyes and saw that flames surrounded the house. Everyone went out of the room except R. Elazar his son and R. Aba. R. Shimon then said to his son: "Go and see if R. Yitzhak is here, for I am responsible for him. Tell him to arrange his affairs and to sit with me. Happy is his lot."

R. Shimon arose, smiled and was happy. He asked: "Where is everyone?" R. Elazar went to assemble them and they sat before him. R. Shimon said: "This is a propitious hour on which I, unashamedly, seek to enter the next world. There are sacred matters hitherto undisclosed. I want to appear before God, without it being said of me that I left the world lacking. Until now, my secrets were in my heart so that I could enter the next world with them. And now, I shall instruct you: R. Aba will write, R. Elazar my son will explain and the rest of the disciples will only meditate."

R. Aba arose behind him and R. Elazar, his son, sat in front of him. That entire day, the fire continued to encircle the house and no one could approach it. I fell to the ground and wept. After the fire ceased, I saw the Holy Light, the Holy of Holies that had departed from this world, lying on his right side, smiling—R. Hiya stood up and said: "Until now, the Holy Light protected us; this is the hour to pay him honour."

They put him on his bed. Only R. Elazar and R. Aba tended him. The officials came to talk to them and the people of Meron rebuked them, for they thought that he would not be buried there. After the bier was taken out, it rose in the air and a fire burned in front of it. A voice was heard: "Come and gather for the Celebration of R. Shimon!"

The mystics who go to Meron on Lag B'Omer feel the full impact of the day and believe that R. Shimon bar Yohai is with them, communicating the hidden meanings of the Torah.

On the eve of Lag B'Omer, the celebrants march forth with an ancient Torah scroll brought from Spain carried in front of them under a decorated canopy. The tradition of the parade and the scroll has been preserved by the Abo family of Safed for many generations. A special torch-lighting ceremony is held in the Abo yard; the torch is brought from Jerusalem, from the top of Mt. Zion, in keeping with the verse: "There shall be light for him from Zion." At the head of the marchers, walk the important people of Safed and the representatives of various groups. The leaders carry the Torah scroll which is decorated with garlands of flowers. They are followed by school-children with the kindled torch and the march is accompanied by joyful sounds. The marchers traverse the streets of Safed singing and dancing; many even play with swords and bows and arrows. They reach Meron towards evening. All day long, motley groups stream to Meron. Everyone presses through the gate into the Burial Chamber where the mystics are sitting and studying the Zohar, as well as other passages associated with the teachings and death of R. Shimon bar Yohai. As the stars appear, the Rabbi of

Safed kindles a bonfire and everyone begins to sing: "Bar Yohai! Bar Yohai!"

Meron resounds with melodies and the sound of singing voices. People dance in circles and play stringed instruments, drums and flutes. They sing and dance in honour of R. Shimon bar Yohai who, according to tradition, is present and rejoices in their joy.

Haircutting

It is customary to bring young children to Meron on Lag B'Omer, in order to cut their hair and to arrange their sidelocks (PEOT). Children are carried on their parents' shoulders to the Chamber opposite the tombs and there their hair is cut, in the midst of singing. The ceremony of "cutting the hair" takes place in the morning and is called by the Arabic name *"Halakah."* Many people weigh the child's hair and give the equivalent weight to charity in coins. While doing so, they utter a special prayer that the lad grow up to study the Torah, marry and perform good deeds.

In the early part of the century, Mr. Y. Goldfarb related: "We went down to the study-room where we were greeted by a fascinating sight: In the midst of the noise and confusion, various Jews assembled. They carried small children, three years old, dressed in neat trousers and clean long coats. On their heads, were round turbans trimmed with golden flax made for the occasion. Under the headcoverings, were bushy curls and uncombed sidelocks. The fathers were distributing wine and "goodies" to everyone who passed by. Then, the sexton of the place approached with scissors in his hand and carefully, while talking gently to the child, began to cut. The child was frightened and began crying but the barber completed his task. When this was done, he blessed the father, saying: "May God help you to raise your son to be a good Jew who will serve the Almighty." Then everyone around began to sing and dance."

In many places, it is customary on Lag B'Omer to take out the school children to forests, to play with bows and arrows. This practice is a reminder of Bar Kochba's rebellion which is associated with Lag B'Omer. Others regard it as stemming from the tradition that no rainbow was seen in the skies in the days of R. Shimon bar Yohai.

IV. TALES AND LEGENDS

There are many stories associated with Meron and Lag B'Omer. Most of them originate with pilgrimage customs, or the Meron way of life. These tales would be told around the bonfire during the Celebration, or by those making the trip to Meron, a trip often lasting several days. Such people often felt the need to explain their undertaking, or wanted to overcome the feeling of danger. Some stories are related in different versions depending on who the story-teller is, or upon the circumstances in which they are told. Those presented here are the stories told by contemporary guides and tourists; some of them are new tales reflecting the new situation.

Miracle Tales

Meron is full of miracles; they are mostly associated with R. Shimon bar Yohai who was regarded by the sages as a specialist in miracles.

A terrible accident occurred in Meron in 5671 (1911). A railing broke and several people fell. Seven were killed outright and four died later in Safed. Nevertheless, people continued to come and the crowds made the situation dangerous. Stories however, were told to calm everyone and to move them to trust in R. Shimon bar Yohai. The sages had said of him: "When hard pressed, it is worth-while relying on R. Shimon."

The Miracle of the Child

R. Haim Halevi Horwitz, author of *Hibbat Yerushalayim*, reads:

"I praise God that I was privileged to be in Meron on Lag B'Omer of 5539 and I will now relate the great miracle which I myself beheld.

It was when everyone, men, women and children had reached the roof of R. Shimon Bar Yohai's Study Hall in order to gaze upon the Celebration, that a five year old child fell down to the ground below. The roof was high up and when the child reached the ground, he was, indeed, like one dead. Those assembled woefully clasped their hands as they murmured: "The child is dead." The father wept and a doctor who was present ordered blood-letting for the boy. Then, the child revived and began crying: "Father!" When the crowd heard the child crying, it returned to the Celebration. The good Lord sent the child a complete recovery and the next day he was completely well. He joined his father in celebrating with everyone. Everyone knew that it was due to the merit of the Holy Teacher that the child had recovered.

Respect for the Righteous

Even the Arabs of the neighborhood regarded the graves of the righteous with awe and were careful not to touch them. They would come near only when they wanted to request divine help in time of trouble. They showed great respect and would tell tales about the holy man buried there. They revered the gravestones, the caves and even the old trees which gave shade and fruit such as carobs, figs and dates. They told stories of miracles about the trees so that they would not be cut down or damaged.

Many of these stories were about the trees at the Cave of Hillel, at the grave of R. Shimon bar Yohai and alongside the grave of R. Yohanan Hasandlar. In connection with the tree at the Cave of Hillel, there was the story of a non-Jew who had cut off two pieces to make a yoke. That night, his wife dreamt that she heard a warning that her husband and two sons would die if the pieces were not returned. When she told her husband the dream, he burst out laughing and paid no heed to her whatsoever. The next day, his two sons fell fatally ill. He then remembered the dream and ran quickly to the cave to pray and to repair the damage.

The sages of Safed who built the study-hall over the grave of R. Shimon bar Yohai told of the governor, a wicked man who hated Jews and who forbade the building to be completed. The sages pleaded with him, in the name of R. Shimon, but he was adamant and refused to acquiesce. That night, he was overcome with trembling. He dreamt of the old and revered Saint coming to him and threatening him: "Who are you to forbid the building of my house?" The governor was terrified and immediately sent a servant to tell the sages to complete the building quickly.

The Arabs of Meron tell of this incident in relation to the grave of R. Yohanan Hasandlar: One of the local Arabs hid his flock in the Cave of R. Yohanan and appointed a young boy to watch over them while he went away. When he came back, he did not find the lad. Then, the youngster returned and the Arab shouted at him and cursed him. The boy said to him: "Do not be afraid. I placed the animals under the protection of the Saint." The Arab began to beat him and to curse the Saint. While he was hitting the boy, the Saint punished him. He contorted his face, twisted his neck around and made him dumb so that he could not open his mouth. The boy hurried to his master's home to tell what had happened. Only after a sacrifice was brought and prayers were said at the grave, did the Saint relent and cure the man. The Arab then vowed to kindle an eternal light at the grave and prepared an oil lamp for the Cave of R. Yohanan Hasandlar. Stories of wonders and miracles were told about this cave and the oil lamp inside.

In respect to the righteous dead, people were careful not to offend the pilgrims, not to insult them nor to take anything from them. They were very careful not to steal at a holy site even though the people who came there often, and, particularly, before the Sabbath when they hid money and articles in a cave, being certain that the holy man buried there, would protect them from thieves. In this connection, many stories were told of thieves who dared to steal and were punished. At the moment they laid their hands on the money or on one of the articles, they would become like a piece of stone, unable to move before being caught.

Many tales tell of those who hesitated about making the pilgrimage at times when crowds did not go to Meron. They were afraid that they would not find a *minyan,* or they were upset by those who mocked the Lag B'Omer Celebration on the anniversary of Bar Yohai's death, contending that it should be a day of mourning. Other scoffers regarded the trip as a waste of time that should be spent in study.

Those Who Complete the Minyan

When special pilgrimages took place, throngs came to Meron in groups; at other times, however, very few visited and there were times when there was only a handful. These men would eagerly search for others in order to round out a *minyan.* There are many stories about those who suddenly appeared to fulfill this role at *minha* time, or for a circumcision or a special event. Just then, these individuals appeared out of nowhere, and they would similarly disappear without leaving a trace. They were generally regarded as members of R. Shimon bar Yohai's inner circle, who were on guard to make certain that the spark of prayer and study would never be extinguished. They made sure therefore, that every pilgrim to Meron would find a *minyan* for services, for reading the

Torah and saying the *kaddish* so that no one need stay away in fear that he would not find the necessary *quorum*.

The story of R. Yehezkel the Hermit is well-known. He lived alone in Meron but whenever he needed a minyan to pray, other Jews suddenly appeared.

Spiritual Pilgrimage

The pilgrimage to Meron is considered a religious command-ment. Those who believe so, reject the view that the time involved should rather be spent in study. They accept the teaching that "the righteous are even greater in death than in life." They feel that the deceased saints are alive in their midst and continue to study and to teach. They maintain that studying at the graves of the righteous enables them to commune with their spirits and to rise to greater spiritual heights.

Many stories were told about scholars who went to Meron and imbibed doctrines and insights from R. Shimon bar Yohai and his circle that were unattainable elsewhere. According to the testimony of R. Haim Vital, the saintly R. Isaac Luria was granted many revelations at the time that he isolated himself in Meron and com-muned with the souls of the righteous. It is related that he once said to his disciples: "If you were only granted the privilege to see, you would view a large band of saints and ministering angels who have come to learn and also the fire burning all about us."

Many stories were told also about simple men who suddenly became learned scholars in Meron. A well known one concerned one of the leading mystics of Safed who had been an ordinary, ignorant person but who became a great scholar, thanks to R. Shi-mon bar Yohai who appeared to him in a dream on Lag B'Omer in Meron and taught him Torah. This is how it happened: this individ-ual once sat in a class in the Zohar. The mystics were sitting in a semi-circle, each one reading and explaining a chapter. When his turn came, he was asked to read. He was deeply embarrassed and burst into tears because he could not read and knew so little. That night, Bar Yohai appeared to him, told him not to grieve and taught him throughout the night.

The next day, everyone again sat in a semi-circle and continued their studies. When this man's turn came, they were afraid to call on him and wanted to pass him by. But he arose and asked permission to read; he did so and explained many matters that had perplexed them. They were all amazed and wondered how he could have acquired such profound comprehension. They would not leave him alone until he told them what had happened with R. Shimon bar Yohai. Henceforth, they showed him great respect and appointed him one of their leaders.

The Promise of the Meron

The mystics believe that the great light shed by R. Shimon bar Yohai, continues to emanate from his resting place to those devoted to his teachings.

When R. Shimon died, a heavy mourning descended on the world and the whole creation was enveloped by it. Different locations vied for his body, and important men from each came to claim it. They placed the body under a canopy and bore it from his room. While they were doing so, the bed itself arose into the air and was surrounded by fire. A voice then resounded throughout the world: "Come! Gather together for the Celebration of R. Shimon!" The bed remained in a hovering position at Meron, over the Cave and everyone understood that this cave was designated for R. Shimon from the beginning of creation.

When he was brought into the cave, a second voice was heard: "Go to rest at last and you will arise to your fate at the end of days." After they buried him in the ground, his disciple R. Hiya, prostrated himself, kissed the earth and wept. R. Hiya became angry at the ground which dared hide the light of the world and rebuked it: "Since you are so audacious, the great light will consume you." The earth thereupon promised him that it would not extinguish the light, hence it still emanates from that spot.

R. Yehuda told it differently: R. Shimon did not remain in the ground but ascended to heaven. The earth was afraid to accept the great light. It endeavoured to keep dampness and worms from the body, but was afraid that it could not. It was so full of worry and apprehension that Heaven took pity. One day, when R. Yehuda was sleeping lightly under a tree, he saw four wings spread out, with R. Shimon ascending upon them. With him, were the Books of Heavenly Secrets.

Ben Shlomo, who generally regards the earth with contempt and dislikes it because of its audacity towards the bodies of the righteous, maintains that the earth was its usual indifferent self even to R. Shimon bar Yohai. It contended: "From earth he came, to earth he will return." It was scalded however, by the strong fire and feared for itself. It turned therefore, to the heavens and agreed to hand him over.

The Plain of Dinars

One of the plains in the vicinity of Meron is associated with a legend that reflects R. Shimon bar Yohai's great attachment to Eretz Yisrael. The legend tells us of one of his disciples who left the country, made a lot of money and returned a wealthy man. This moved others to want to do likewise. When R. Shimon heard about this, he was apprehensive lest they prove unable to withstand temptation. He, thereupon, invited them to accompany him to this plain. When they reached it, he ordered the plain to fill up with *dinars*, and it obeyed to do so. He turned to his disciples and said: "If you want gold, there it is in front of you! Know you however, that every measure you take will be deducted from your share in the World-to-Come." Thereupon the disciples rejected the golden *dinars* and never touched them again.

The Serpent, Guardian of the Graves

The stories of the serpent guarding the graves are very interesting. Whereas the snake is ordinarily pictured as an evil creature that bites and causes damage, it is not portrayed this way in regard to the graves in Meron. There, it is pictured as doing good by protecting the graves from harm. In the tales of Meron, the serpent is found particularly as the guardian of the graves of R. Yohanan Hasandlar and R. Shimon bar Yohai.

R. Shimon had been a recluse most of his life, spending his time in studying Torah. Hence was he kept apart from others in death. His followers did not allow anyone to be buried alongside him and the serpent guarded the entrance to the cave. When they brought his son R. Elazar, there, it rose to its full stature and refused to allow anyone to enter until they whispered: "Serpent! Serpent! Open your mouth and let the son enter to be next to his father!" This he did.

There was a similar incident with R. Yitzhak Napha who was buried in the vicinity of the Cave of R. Shimon, but outside the entrance to his grave. When he was being carried to his burial place, the serpent rose up and refused to allow them to come near. Those accompanying the body told him what R. Yitzhak had done for R. Shimon (as related in mystic lore), and the serpent could not decide what to do. He could not defy them but neither could he permit them to enter. He, therefore, encircled the cave and lay inert. Since the sages could not pass him by, they buried R. Yitzhak nearby, outside the cave.

The serpent had decided on the burial-place for both R. Elazar and R. Yitzhak. When the time came to bury R. Shimon's grandson, R. Yosi, the serpent would not budge. The sages almost came to blows with him, but trouble was averted by the intervention of a Heavenly Voice.

R. Yosi, son of R. Elazar, was a great man in his day. He was as good as he was learned, beloved by God and man. When he died, a large funeral was arranged and he was brought to Meron, to the cave of his father and grandfather. But the serpent was coiled about the entrance and the sages wanted to move him by force. When they said: "Serpent! Serpent! Open up and let the son approach his father," he refused. He blocked the entrance with his tail in his mouth. Those gathered around began to murmur and were prepared to move him forcibly. One of the elders, however, stopped them and told them how loyal the serpent was to R. Shimon and his son. They were not convinced; they felt it would be disrespectful to R. Yosi not to inter him in the cave. They glared at the serpent in anger and he looked at them in sorrow. He obviously wanted to say something to them, but was not able. Then a miracle occurred and a Heavenly Voice was heard saying: "Not because one is greater than the other, but because one suffered in the cave when hiding from the persecutors of his people, while the other did not." At once, they parted amicably and buried R. Yosi in his place.

The Dwelling Place of the World

The day after Lag B'Omer, the curator saw a Jew, obviously a new immigrant, standing with his family and belongings alongside the grave of R. Yitzhak Napha outside the Cave. He was praying with great fervour and seemed to be arguing with the deceased. The curator went up to him and asked for what he was praying. The man replied that he was a new immigrant who had just arrived from

North Africa. He could not find a place to live and had to keep moving from place to place; so he came to the grave of R. Yitzhak Napha to pray for a place where to live. The curator asked him why he chose R. Yitzhak Napha as his intercessor in Heaven.

The man replied that, when he was in North Africa he had learned, in the name of R. Yitzhak Napha, that God was the Dwelling-Place of the world. "Moses said in the Torah: 'The eternal God is a dwelling place'" (Deut. 33:27). That verse however, did not make it clear whether God was the dwelling-place of the world, or that the world was His dwelling-place. Then came R. Yitzhak bar Napha and informed us that the verse "O Lord, Thou art a dwelling place" teaches that God is the dwelling-place of the world. I learned this from him and taught it to others. So, when I came to Eretz Yisrael and could not find a roof for my family, I came to his grave to talk to him. I came with a complaint: "If God is the dwelling-place of the world and I am part of the world, then my dwelling-place is in God. I came therefore, to demand my home in the dwelling-place of the world."

The curator commented: "You are right" and added: "For years and years, we have come to the grave of R. Yitzhak Napha to pray and to request a dwelling for Israel from the Dwelling-Place of the World." He then began investigating a home for the immigrant and found him one in Kfar Shammai, not far from R. Yitzhak Napha.

The Shofar under the Chair

The mystics speak of the Chair of Elijah hovering over the hills of Meron and overlooking Galilee. This chair was prepared for him so he could look out upon the Plain of Arbael and announce the Messiah when he comes. The chair is prepared but the prophet is not seated on it. He is wandering about the universe helping those in need, and the chair is empty.

Under the chair a shofar is buried. It is not Elijah's shofar, but one belonging to R. Shimon bar Yohai. It was hidden in his Study-House, until a mysterious stranger came and withdrew it without permission. This is recorded in books according to the sages of Safed. It was at a most difficult time for Jewry. The mystics met secretly to hasten the Redemption and bring Salvation. They scattered to all the places where certain things were to be done. One of them, who remained anonymous, went to Meron to the resting place of R. Shimon, who will have a role to play during the period of the coming of the Messiah.

What did he do? He isolated himself in the synagogue in Meron. He fasted and afflicted himself; he purified himself seven times in the spring near Meron and recited special prayers. On Yom Kippur, he joined those who met in the burial chamber, to pour out their hearts and he stood all day long on his feet, his face radiant. Towards evening, when all were reciting the closing prayers, he secretly took the Shofar that was under the Ark and rushed from the yard to the valley underneath. He leapt from stone to stone, until he came to the top of the hill, to the rock called "Elijah's Chair," the place where Elijah will stand and blow the Shofar. When the congregation finished the closing service, they heard the sound of the Shofar echoing through the hills. They went to the place where it had been sounded and found the mystic stretched out at the base of the Chair, his huge hands grasping the Shofar and his head turned upward. They wanted to bury him right there, but those who knew the law protested that because Elijah was a priest, he could not be so defiled. As they were afraid to take the Shofar back, they hid it underneath the chair where it remains to this day.

When the Clouds Scatter

Just before Lag B'Omer in 1945, at the end of World War II, the curator then a boy in his father's home, went to the kindling of the fire in Meron with the elders of Jerusalem. The ascent was not easy and even somewhat dangerous. They arrived on time, met in the different chambers, studied selections from the Zohar, prayed with intense devotion and prepared the bonfire. When the time came, they accompanied the Rabbi of Safed to the roof singing as they did so, in order to arrange everything. The sky was overcast and neither the moon nor the stars could be seen.

One of the veteran mystics thought it wise to delay the kindling because of the clouds which covered the skies and said: "We kindle the fire at night after the heavens light up for us, light facing light, the lower light opposite the upper light. But if there is no light in the heavens, why kindle? Let us wait for the clouds to scatter, so that the light from below can unite with that above."

They waited some time, but the clouds did not disperse. In the meantime, people were streaming to the roof and waiting. At first, they waited patiently, but then they lost patience. They wanted to start and the Rabbi of Safed took a bottle of oil in his hand; but the old man intervened, stopped the kindling and begged them to wait for the clouds to scatter. Out of respect to him, there was no alternative but to wait. The people were upset and tense, but they waited. After a while, everyone began buzzing with excitement; someone had just come from Tel Aviv with news. "It was announced over the radio just now," he said, "that Hitler, may his name be blotted out, has committed suicide." The old mystic pushed his way to the place of the bonfire and said: "The clouds have dispersed. Let the lower lights leap forth to the upper lights." Then was the fire kindled with hearty singing and dancing that went on until daybreak.

R. Shmuel the Kindler

R. Shmuel was in the habit of going from Safed to Meron every Friday afternoon to light candles at the grave of the saintly R.

Shimon bar Yohai. There was nothing that could keep him from this practice, he was called therefore "R. Shmuel the Kindler."

In those days, it was dangerous to go from Safed to Meron because of the robbers and animals that abounded. In the winter, there were heavy rains and difficult Galilean snows; in the summer, the heat was stifling. None of this however, kept R. Shmuel from going to R. Shimon's grave for ten years. He never missed kindling his candle at the grave for even one Friday afternoon.

About fifty years ago, during a difficult winter when snow fell all week and all the roads were carpeted with white, it seemed impossible to go up to Meron. The local Arabs then said to each other: "This time, the Jew will not come to light his candles." R. Shmuel, however, would not forego his sacred task and he went forth as always, even though all that he could see before him was snow and still more snow. His feet sank into it but he plodded on undaunted. When the Arabs of Meron stared toward Safed, they were utterly amazed to see a small, dark dot advancing toward them. It was, to their great surprise, R. Shmuel the Kindler and they could not believe their eyes.

R. Shmuel went into the courtyard and, as always, approached Bar Yohai's grave to light the candle, but he was unable to open the gate because of the snowdrifts which had accumulated thereon. R. Shmuel strained and exerted himself to remove the large piles in order to open the gate. While he was doing this, stopping only to wipe the sweat off his forehead and from his eyes, another Jew appeared. R. Shmuel did not know him but he too began removing the snow. Then a miracle occurred! As the stranger touched the snow, it melted as if many bonfires had been lit. It then became possible to open the gate with ease.

The stranger opened it and said that he had feared that no one was coming to light the candle at the grave of R. Shimon bar Yohai; he had therefore, come to do so himself. R. Shmuel was astounded at the fact that another Jew observed, as he did, this custom and wanted to learn something about him. First, he entered the chamber, lit the candles and put them in their usual place, then, he went outside to look for the stranger but was amazed to find that he had disappeared.

He searched and searched, but was not successful. So, he set out on his way back to Safed. It was extremely difficult for him to do so, and the hour was late. Snowflakes continued to fall from the gray skies and he was afraid that he would not get back in time before the onset of the Sabbath. His heart beat furiously and he was concerned that they would worry about him at home if he did not get back on time, thereby marring their Sabbath peace. But how could he get back when the sun was already setting, the roads covered with snow and he was so weary?

He became even more distressed when he heard sounds of the wild animals who were emerging from their lairs. Indeed, his blood froze from within him. He began to sweat from weariness and nervousness but, nevertheless he trusted in God and prayed to Him to save him. He lifted his eyes in prayer and said: "Father in Heaven, please help me and save me, for the sake of the righteous R. Shimon bar Yohai who studied and taught Torah for the sake of Your name and to give You pleasure."

Just as he finished his prayer, there appeared the stranger who had made such a profound impression by his noble bearing and white beard. The man invited him to accompany him. R. Shmuel the Kindler was pleased and went along. The stranger walked in front and once again, the same miracle occurred: wherever he set down his foot, the snow melted at once. Moreover, the walking became easier and quicker; it seemed no effort to plod on as if indeed, the ground was leaping from under them.

In a short while, he was in his own yard and in his pleasant, warm home in Safed. R. Shmuel the Kindler rejoiced over God's great miracle and thanked him with all his heart, soul and might. He entered his home singing praises of God Who is good and Who does good. He wanted to invite the elderly stranger into his home for the Sabbath, but he had disappeared once again. That night, R. Shmuel dreamt that the old man was sitting on the Chair of Elijah at the top of the mountain and smiling at him while his face shone with goodness.

The Mysterious Dance

Dancing on Lag B'Omer at Meron is an integral part of the Celebration. It is done in a circle, hand on shoulders, with great ardour and enthusiasm. Most interesting is the story of the Mysterious Dance whereby R. Elazar Azkari (author of *Haredim*) revealed himself:

The mystics relate that R. Elazar was a shy, retiring man and no one knew of his great learning and righteous deeds. When he was the sexton in the synagogue, they treated him as an ordinary man. He went once with the disciples of Isaac Luria to Meron on Lag B'Omer and danced with them at the Celebration. Suddenly, a very distinguished old man, dressed in white, appeared. He took R. Elazar by the hand and began to dance with him alone with great fervor and enthusiasm. The two danced on with religious devotion. Everyone looked and was amazed. The disciples could not figure out who the old man was who had appeared so suddenly. They looked at him with awe. R. Isaac Luria, who had been standing aside, lost in thought, came up to the two dancers, put one hand on the stranger and one on R. Elazar and danced with them in a circle. They whirled around with great joy and religious concentration. The disciples were astounded that their master would dance with the simple sexton and finally decided to ask him for an explanation. "We can understand the master's dancing with the mysterious old man. We do not know who he is but he must be a great man. We cannot, however, understand how you could dance with the sexton,

Elazar. Is it proper for you to leave your disciples and to dance with him with such tremendous enthusiasm?"

Rabbi Luria smiled and replied: "If R. Shimon bar Yohai could dance with him alone, is it not proper for me, who is younger, to do the same?" Since then, R. Elazar became an honoured person in the eyes of the mystics and they treated him with awe and reverence.

The Kindling on Mt. Zion

On the morning of Lag B'Omer of 1950, the curator arranged for a fire to be quickly kindled in the courtyard of the tomb of King David on Mt. Zion. The elders were surprised and asked him: "What is the purpose of this fire? Competition with Meron? Is this, in addition to Meron? Or is it, perhaps, in place of the fire which used to be kindled in Jerusalem at the cave of Shimon the Righteous?"

"None of these" answered the curator. "It is because of the 'notes.' Pilgrims to Mt. Zion leave "notes" at the tomb or place them into the cracks between the stones, according to the Hassidic practice. These "notes" contain prayers for health, success in business, a good match, protection from all evil, long life for the family, and so on. Some make religious requests for complete redemption, greater understanding of the Torah, to be able to see the hidden light and to bask in the splendour of the Divine Presence, and so on. The "notes" remain on the tomb for a few days, then fall off and are trodden on by visitors. I wondered what to do!"

The curator went on to say that he had gone to his saintly father and asked him to take care of the "notes." The Rabbi refused and said: "We are the descendants of R. Haim of Valozhin who opposed the whole business of "notes," and hence we have no right to have anything to do with them." He next turned to a noted Hassidic rabbi and asked him to examine the "notes" and to pray for the fulfillment of the prayers they contained. He refused, saying: "Who am I to deal with "notes" given to King David?"'

In the meanwhile, the stacks of "notes" were accumulating. They were all over the tomb and visitors began reading them and making jokes about them. This upset the curator greatly and he had to decide what to do. One of the old men who spend their days on Mt. Zion suggested that he take them to Meron on Lag B'Omer and offer them up as petitions in the fire of Bar Yohai. This would be in keeping with the practice of reciting petitionary prayers and with the belief that the time of the fire is very propitious.

The curator accepted the suggestion, collected all the notes on the floor of the room of King David's tomb and took them to Meron. He put them at the base of the fire and, when they went up in flames, he recited the traditional prayer that they ascend to heaven for the sake of R. Shimon bar Yohai and be accepted there with love. As the petitions rose on high, a smile of joy spread over the curator's face. When he told the mystics of Safed about this, they were not pleased. They did not approve of his bringing petitions from Mt. Zion, for Mt. Zion is the gateway to Heaven and lies opposite the Gate of Prayers to which King David has the keys. They agreed that the "notes" should ascend in fire, but they disapproved of the place. They advised him to kindle the Lag B'Omer fire on Mt. Zion, whence the prayers could rise directly through the Gate to the Entrance Hall of the Temple of Prayer. The curator was very moved and returned at once to Jerusalem. He gathered the rest of the "notes" and offered them up there, so that they could go directly through the Gate to the Entrance Hall of Heaven.

TRACES OF NOAH'S ARK IN GALILEE

The Bible gives detailed dimensions of the Ark Noah was asked to construct, its dimensions, how long it took in building, and how long it would continue to float on the waters of the Flood. The main problem is where it had stopped floating after the waters had subsided; the Torah just succinctly tells us that "the Ark rested on the Seventh month, on the seventeenth day thereof, near Mt. Ararat."

Historians have ever been intrigued to find out exactly where the spot was, and archaeologists tired not in sending out one expedition after another in order to discover traces of the Ark. Since it was so high, and so firmly built across a span of so many years, surely a trace of its existence must still survive. Even the discovery of a nail or a screw would be most welcome. And so the quest goes on to this day to discover the slightest traces of the Ark. The main problem is: Where is Mt. Ararat? Some have opined that this mountain is in the region of the Caucasian mountains, in Armenia, Iraq and in many other places. To this day, the mountain has remained unidentified, and not the slightest clue of the Ark has been discovered. It still baffles all; but the search still goes on.

Many years ago, such an expedition visited Israel on its way to America and the Caucuses. They remained here for several weeks, scanned every likely place where it could have rested, and conducted many a conversation with various learned archaeologists, historians, and biblical scholars, in the hope of discovering the slightest trace. The learned scholars of Israel smilingly listened to their arguments, answering all their searching questions with a patient shrug of the shoulders; as if to say: "Queer people these!

Are they mentally balanced?'' Loudly they told them that as they had no clue themselves, they could not help them in their quest.

The expedition leaders also met the Director of the Holy Places in Israel, in the hope that he might be of help to them. His reputation had reached them and they were advised that it would be worth their while to discuss the whole matter with him, since he was at home in all the old sources, both talmudic, midrashic and cabbalistic, he might be able to help them. So they came to see him to discuss with him Noah's Ark and the possibility of tracing its whereabouts. The Director also heard them politely, with a smile on his lips, for this was not the first time—nor seemingly would it be the last—that such questions would be fired at him. At the end of the interview, however, he became more serious, promising them to show them some remains of that Ark.

"You are mocking us," they turned to him in sheer disbelief at his promise.

"What makes you think so?" he replied. "Is this not what you are looking for? and is not the cause that brought you all this way here to Israel. I am serious, I will show you some traces of the Ark.

They were taken to Galilee and shown around the new settlements, *Ma'abarat* and villages, machanot and Kibbutzim, where they met new immigrants from the world over—from Poland, Roumania, Hungary, Morocco, who had only just come over, brought direct from the ship to their new homes. In the glare of the blazing sun, these new homesteads were set up, having large families, and protected only from the elements by wooden or tin huts. They beheld half-naked builders, perspiring and fatigued, building these modest homes with hammer and trowel, nail and bolt.

They went from one *ma'abarat* to another, full of admiration and wonder at what their eyes beheld, none spoke a word and none offered a question. They strictly kept their promise. As night succeeded the day, they came home, satisfied at what they have seen.

When the day came to its end, they sat in the small room of the Director, which was littered with papers and notices which he collected from all over the world, so that he might be apprised of what is transpiring in the Jewish world. Then he began to tell his guests the meaning of his conducted tours over the length and breadth of the Galilee.

You were perplexed when I showed you all these new settlements when I promised to show you the remains of Noah's Ark. But actually, I did. The Bible is the history of mankind written thousands of years in advance. Its stories are eternal, always actual. These new immigrants you have seen, orphans saved from the hellish concentration camps, and the wrath of a hostile world, these are the relics of Noah's Ark. These are the pathetic, but glorious remains of the Flood of murderous hatred which Hitler and his Nazis forth into the world. The diabolical, fiendish gang have disappeared, but what you have seen today are the living relics of what, let us hope, is a buried past."

I bring you to the Galilee because in the Galilee we begin the last hundred years to build the Ark of Noah of our generation and we build this at the eternal light of the great cabalist Bar Yohai who saves the world from deluge and shows everyone the way to the Ark Legend.

Legend has it that, so saintly was this learned Rabbi during his lifetime that the rainbow never appeared to illumine the Heavens and to reassure the world of God's protection, because the spiritual light diffused by this holy man was so brilliant and powerful that it was sufficient shield against the darkness of a second deluge.

Although he was a man of marked and profound humility, the Rabbi was once heard to say that in unison with the radiance shed by the son of Uzziah, Jotham, he could hold the whole earth in safety from its commencement to its final destiny.

This was a saying hard to understand. What was this light spread around by Jotham? It was the glowing lamp of filial love and obedience to the Fifth Commandment. Uzziah had the terrible misfortune to become a leper, but the love and respect of his son did not grow less; rather, with infinite compassion, it increased.

As his father was now unable to rule his Kingdom, Jotham ruled in his stead; but it was a rule of proxy only. Everything that was done, every law passed, every edict uttered, was promulgated by Jotham but issued in the name of King Uzziah. The government was by the selfless and hidden rule of the son, but the Kingship and Majesty continued as that of the father.

It was the bright flame of such honouring of his father, which rendered Jotham fit to be the guardian of all humanity. Such nobility was strong enough to save the earth from all the powers of annihilation. Of such magnitude is veneration and reverence for father and mother and the family circle, that it is the very life-blood of security and prosperity for all mankind.

As the Director concluded his explanation, the truth dawned upon his heaven. They now understood, and were all the wiser for the new light that was now shed on their quest. The Lesson? The Jewish Bible is a Book of Life, not like the Egyptian "Book of the Dead." So why search for bolts and screws of a wrecked Ark in the neighborhood of an unknown Ararat, when all around us are living relics of those saved from a modern flood and brought to the Ark of Medinat Israel at the light of Bar Yohai.

WEDDINGS ON LAG BA'OMER

In the days of the Temple, Jewish men brought an offering of their first barley-harvest, on the second day of Pesach; and the following forty-nine days, counted until the Festival of Shavuot, were numbered as the Days of the Omer (or prescribed quantity of grain). These seven weeks were called Sefirah; and the period was kept as a king of semi-mourning, when Observant Jews abstained from certain celebrations and among them that of marriage. On the thirty-third day of Omer, known as Lag Ba'Omer, however, this restriction was lifted, and it became indeed a very popular day for weddings. There are various explanations for the exemption from mourning on the thirty-third day: one is that a devastating pestilence was halted on Lag Ba'Omer; another, that it ended on that day.

There is a story about the holy Rabbi Shimon ben Yohai, who loved to act as a benevolent marriage counsellor, and bring together again married couples who had fallen away from each other; and to conciliate those who had quarrelled: that one day a husband and wife stood before him, and sadly asked him to arrange for a divorce between them. Gently and kindly, he questioned them, and found that their trouble was not lack of affection (for they still loved each other dearly), but lack of any children, for whom they both longed.

The Rabbi heard them to the end, and then gave his counsel, and bade them end their marriage as they had begun it—with a festival and celebration. It seemed to be a gay and happy occasion; there was good wine and healths were drunk. In his speech to the assembled company, the husband spoke with generous appreciation and gratitude of his wife and all that she had been to him; and as a final gesture bade her take to her new home, as a memento of her former life, whatever treasure she would like best to keep beside her.

Later in the evening, after more copious rounds of wine, the husband fell fast asleep; and seizing her opportunity, the wife called on her friends to pick him up and take him to the house where she would henceforth be living. In the morning the husband awakened, startled and confused at his unfamiliar surroundings. Finding his wife still beside him bewildered him still more, and he begged to know where he was, and why he was there! Tenderly, his wife made answer that when he bade her choose a memento to take away with her, she had chosen HIM, as the sweetest Keepsake she could ever want or have! Overcome with his memories of their many loving years together, the husband cancelled the divorce— and they lived happily ever after.

Since that time tells R. Yehuda Leib of Poltishn that it was customary in Meron for barren people to pray for children. If their prayers were answered, they would give charity, come to Meron to thank God and have the child's first haircut there. Barren women often prostrated themselves on the grave of R. Shimon bar Yohai as they prayed for offspring. Simple women believe that the very act of prostrating.

Thereupon Rabbi Shimon prayed for them and the woman bore a child.

Why did he not pray for them before? As long as they wanted to follow the strict interpretation of the law, there was no place for mercy. However, once they went beyond the law, R. Shimon could say to Go: "Now, You deal with them *beyond* the law."

That is why Hannah did not go to pray for a child from the Lord until her husband, Elkaneh, had said: "Am I not better to you than ten sons?"

THE LEGENDARY LINTEL OF MIRON

Lag B'omer is a day dedicated to the anniversary of the death of R. Simeon B. Yochai, the mystic whose mortal remains repose in Miron. Thousands of Jews proceed on pilgrimage there, where huge bonfires are kindled around his tomb, while the whole night is spent in singing and dancing.

Reb Zanwill the curator has spared neither time nor labor around every holy burial place in Israel, and especially at the one in Miron. For this quiet spot was not originally adapted for the scene of such huge pilgrimages. In times gone by, pilgrimages to Miron were also not unknown, but these were infinitessimally small in comparison to those that take place in our days, being the modest affairs by groups of pious people, of mystic bent, who come in asses and small carriages known by the French name of *dilligence*. During the English mandatory regime, a few thousand pilgrims made their annual appearance, but the numbers now approach the 100,000 mark. Hence preparations had to be made to accommodate such vast numbers; roads had to be constructed where none existed before, and these had to be provided with lights, so that no accidents occur on them, besides taking into consideration human needs and hygienic necessities.

A pilgrimage to Miron was always fraught with danger, and this fear was met with the talmudic maxim that "one can safely rely on R. Simeon (B. Johai) in times of emergency." This emergency for which safety was required was especially apparent during the *Hadlakah* (the kindling of the gigantic bonfires). Whereas the Director yields to none in his belief in miracles and in the intervention of R. Simeon, yet he would emphasize the rabbinic dictum that "one must not pin his faith to miracles." G-d helps those who help themselves as it is in the mitzvah of help.

One of the lurking dangers besetting Miron was the legendary lintel of Miron, around which controversy grew acrimonious when it was first marked that it needed strengthening. What sort of lintel was it, and why did such a bitter conflict of opinion grow around it?

On the crest of Miron, above the holy graves, and on a mound by itself once stood the synagogue in which R. Simeon B. Yochai worshipped and which he had made for this purpose. This house of prayer was renowned for its beauty of architecture, and to it many flocked for devotion. In the course of time, it shared the fate of all their synagogues in Galilee, and only heaps of stones remained as witnesses of a glory no longer there. Yet, all was not destroyed; there remained the door-post and the lintel, under which the Mezuzah still was visible. This consisted of a long, firm stone split in two, remaining suspended over the two sides of the entrance; and when Miron was re-conditioned to receive in safety the thousands who now flocked to it, it was also deemed advisable to render this lintel also safe that it fall not on those who pass by. This met with bitter opposition on account of the legend which related that when the lintel fell, Messiah would appear. This remarkable legend, the origin of which is uncertain, has given rise to many tales bordering on the fictitious than on the historical.

The Director is inclined to favour the legend that its origin is based on the belief that the priests of Yehoiriv's family, who delivered the Temple to the Romans when the latter captured Jerusalem, fled for refuge to the wastes of Miron. This belief is expressed in the liturgical poems of R. Eleazur Haklir and R. Pinhas. "They have delivered the House of G-d, and these sons of Jehoiriv, who did so, fled to Miron in Galilee.

There they sit and wait for a sign to return to the temple, knowing that when their synagogue in Miron is also destroyed, it would sound the signal for them to go back to their original home— the Temple. The Director also quotes another current legend which says that Elijah, with his Shofar in hand, sits waiting among the ruins and hills of Miron in order to be able to announce the coming of the Messiah, and to summon the priests of Jehoirib to return to their former duties in the Temple about to be rebuilt. According to these popular beliefs, Miron would be the focal point of the Messianic Age, for it would dawn from those mystic hills which surround it. The mystics who have made their home in Safed and Miron are of the opinion that this legend is associated with the life of Moses. Why?

They believe that in the soul of R. Simeon B. Yochai there sparked a glow of the soul of the Lawgiver, the faithful shepherd of the Jewish people. For just as Moses taught the people the written Law, so did R. Simeon B. Yochai reveal to them the cabbalistic Law, in which are enshrined the deepest meanings of the Torah. In fact, they point thirty identical things which associate the two in partnership. They further point out the numerical value of the word "Lag Bomer," Lamed, Gimel, Beys, Ayin, Mem, Reysh, has a numerical value of three hundred forty-five. Lamed is thirty, Gimel = three, Beys = two, Ayin = seventy, Mem = forty, and Reysh = two hundred, a total of three hundred forty-five. The same as the word MOSHE, the Mem, is forty, the Shin is three hundred, and the Hey is five, also a total of three hundred and forty-five. Also, the day of Lag Bomer always falls on the same day of the week as Zayen Adar, seven days in the month of Adar which is the day of birth and the Yahrzeit of Moses. Therefore they believe that the Beam of Miron that was set aside as a sign of redemption has a connection with the beam of Moses at the time of the redemption of the Israelites from Egypt. In the time of Moses the beam also served as a sign of redemption, as is written in the Torah (Shemos 12:22-23): "And He will see the blood on the beam and on the two door posts, and G-d will pass over the door and will not allow the destroyer to come." The blood on the beam was the good sign that when G-d saw the blood on the beam, He did not permit the destroyer to come into that house.

When they were about to reinforce the beam over the entrance in Miron, the mystics came to the curator of the holy places and claimed: "Curator, what do you intend to do? Enforce, the beam so it shall not fall and thereby hold back, G-d forbid, the redemption, the coming of the Messiah? Or, on the contrary, let the beam fall and thus, according to the legend, hasten the redemption." The curator was puzzled and found himself in a very peculiar position. What to do? Not to hold back the redemption and thereby place the lives of innocent people in danger, or enforce the beam and withhold the redemption? What to do? That was his problem. Which is more important?

A few days later, when the mystics again came to him, he told them that he had decided to enforce the beam. "what! Hold back the redemption?" they exclaimed. "G-d forbid!" the curator told them. "This will hasten the redemption." In order to explain the meaning of his words, he related to them the story that is told about the holy Baal Shem Tov who did much to bring the redemption. King Mesiah, already had packed his belongings and even rented a small boat to bring him to the Holy Land in order to cause the coming of the Mesiah from there. He traveled far on the way to the Holy Land, but at the end he returned and gave up the idea of being instrumental in bringing the Mesiah. Why? Because he was given a sign from heaven that before the coming of the Mesiah, Jews will suffer tortures and terrible edicts. Therefore, his warm heart broke, and he felt that he would be unable to witness Jews' suffering pains. Very dear, was a Jewish life to him, even the life of one individual

Jew. He, therefore, returned to his old home and gave up the thought of bringing the Mesiah. He ran back, his heard did not allow him to see a Jew suffer the pains that he was foretold.

"Here, also," the curator assured the mystics, "when the redemption will be about to take place and the Mesiah will be ready to come, the beam will fall down by itself. The iron door posts will not hold back the Mesiah. The redemption is stronger than iron, and will break the iron. On the other hand, if the beam will not be reinforced, and fall down someday, G-d forbid, over the heads of innocent visitors who come here trusting the great Tzadik Rabbi Shimeon Bar Yocnai, if this large stone should fall on them and kill them, that would hold back the redemption and the coming of the Mesiah. "PIKUACH NEFESH," the saving of souls is greater than anything else in life, even the life of only one person. Saving the lives of many people stands above anything else."

The result was that the beam in Miron was reinforced and made solid. The Mekibulim not only agreed to the work, but they themselves rolled up their sleeves and helped with the reinforcing of the ancient stone, being convinced that saving the lives of human beings is the most important thing in this world, and in the merit of this great deed, the redemption and the arrival of the Mesiah in our time will be hastened.

THE LEGEND OF "ZAPLAG"

The mystic meaning of Bar Yohai's Celebration lies in the staff and light of Moses. On Lag B'Omer therefore, we sing the song: "Be Gracious to us, O Lord, be gracious for the sake of Moses, our Master; Moses is the Faithful Shepherd upon whom the Divine Presence rested." On the anniversaries of Moses' birth and death, both of which are on the seventh of Adar, pilgrimages are also made to Meron.

The relationship of the Faithful Shepherd and R. Shimon bar Yohai is indicated in a number of ways. One consists of connecting the Hebrew letter for seven, ZAYIN, with LAG which equals thirty-three. The day on which the seventh [ZAYIN] of Adar falls, the day of the Faithful Shepherd is the same day of the week that Lag B'Omer, the day of Bar Yohai, falls. ZAYIN [seven] and LAG [thirty-three] alludes to the forty days Moses spent on high receiving all the secrets of the Torah. Hence the practice of going to Meron on the seventh of Adar and on Lag B'Omer, to visit the grave of Bar Yohai and to commune with the spirit of the Faithful Shepherd. You can now understand, in part, the meaning of ZAPLAG—*sayin* [seven] and *lag* [thirty-three] equal forty.

The PEI [eighty] which is added to them is twice MEM [forty]. This refers to the forty-day period Moses twice spent to receive the Torah. Then, there is something else: it is known that Israel accepted the Torah twice. One time was in the days of Moses; the other was in the days of Mordecai and Esther, as the sages said: "They observed it and received it." They observed what they already had and also received the Torah again. The *PEI* is for

Purim. Thus, *ZAPLAG* stands for the three days which occur on the same day of the week: the seventh of Adar, Purim, and Lag B'Omer." See the story about the lintel of Miron.

This alphabetical cleverness amused us but we did not take it seriously. We regarded it as a social game. When the old man noticed our smiles, he went on: "This is no mere game or amusement. What I just told you about ZAPLAG is merely the outer shell of a mystic doctrine. There is also an inner kernel.

If God revealed to Moses the secrets of the Torah, why were these transmitted to Bar Yohai and not to other mystics? We have learned that the concealed is contained in disclosing and revealing names. Moses said to God" "Erase me from your book"; hence, his name was erased from the section read in the synagogue (TET-ZAVEH) during the week of the seventh of Adar (it is read then if it is not a leap year)—either the Saturday before or the Saturday after. Once Moses' name was erased from that section, other parts associated with it also disappeared and they have been hidden away. That was when Moses turned to the mysteries and it, too, involves a deep secret."

The old man stopped for a few moments as if to decide whether or not to continue. Soon, he perked up, took out a piece of paper, wrote something on it and showed those in the room the letters of Moses' name: MEM, SHIN, HEI [Moshe]. Then he said: "Let's see: the revealed aspect of Moses—MEM, SHIN, HEI—was erased from the section of the week of the seventh of Adar. But the undisclosed aspect of the full name of Moses, i.e. only part of his name— MEM [which equals 40], NUN of SHIN [which equals 60], and ALEPH [the last letter of HEI which equals 1]—amounts to 101. That is the numerical value of the angel Michael [the letters of his name equal 101] who is a kind of Moses-on-high. There are 101 verses in the section, TETZAVEH, which equals the number of the concealed Moses. This teaches that all that was omitted was the revealed Moses. The concealed Moses became an unknown part of that section, just as Moses himself was taken above and became part of the secrets of the world, the hidden that awaits discovery, as the Torah says that "no one knew his burial place to this day."

Just as Moses concealed himself on the seventh of Adar, so did the Holy One Blessed-be-He, measure for measure. Purim occurs the week after the seventh of Adar, at the end of the seven day mourning period for Moses. That is the day of the double *mem,* the *pei* of ZAPLAG, the day on which Moses received the second Tablets and when Israel accepted the second Torah. G-d's name is not specifically mentioned in the Scroll of Esther and this also is a concealment. That is why the seventh of Adar and purim occur on the same day of the week. it was Bar Yohai who brought to light the hidden connections between them. He, too, was obligated to keep this secret; that is why he stayed in the cave for 13 years. This then, is the connection with Lag B'Omer, the day of his Celebration which also occurs on the same day of the week. That is the secret of *ZAPLAG* which unites these days and reveals what is hidden."

When he had finished, the old man took us outside, pointed to the bonfire and said: "The bush which Moses saw was burning and, on Lag B'Omer, Jewish children light bonfires; but the time has not yet come to reveal that secret." He finished talking, walked away and vanished.

MERON AND PEKI'IN

Peki'in is connected with Meron. PEKI'IN has a charm all its own which few other villages can equal, let alone excel. It lies nestled among hills and dales, haunted by legends that bear the impress of antiquity and piety; legends which tell of sorrow and joy, life and death, heavenly visitations and of miraculous, heroic happenings. It is especially unique in the sense that it is *sui generis,* being the *only* place in the whole of Eretz-Israel that has never been deserted by Jewish inhabitants since the destruction of Jerusalem by the Romans in 70 C.E. Hunted and haunted, hated and baited, driven and exiled from everywhere else in the Holy Land, Jews never deserted Peki'in, braving the persecutions of their Roman, Persian, Mongolian, Turkish and Arabian despotic masters and overlords.

Throughout the eventful procession of years, some isolated families clung on tenaciously to the village, continuing to forge links in the golden chain of light and shade, joy and sorrow, pride, loyalty and dauntless courage in the face of terrors that flew by day and night.

To this very day, one sole remaining Jewish family— ZAITUM by name, refuses to be dislodged from these sacred haunts; bravely and proudly prolonging the unbroken traditions of PEKI'IN. Tradition records that Rabbi Shimon bar Johai and his son Rabbi Eleazar, found refuge in a cave in PEKI'IN wherein they lived for thirteen years, hidden from the cruel attention of the Romans who had sentenced them to death on account of their being leaders in the Jewish insurrection and their active participation therein!

Reparation to Peki'in

R. Shimon bar Yohai was an active participant in the Revolt against Rome and personally witnessed thousands being put to death by the oppressor, including the flaying of R. Akiba, his sainted master. He opposed the Romans and their rule with every fibre of his being and came out openly against them and their way of life. The Romans sought to imprison him but he always managed to evade capture. At first, he and his son hid in the study-house and his wife daily brought them bread and water. When conditions worsened, he felt that the hiding-place was not safe enough. He said to his son: "Women are lightheaded; the authorities will torture her and she will tell." They thereupon left the study-house and hid in a concealed cave in Peki'in, home of recluses from all over the country. No one knew where they were, except Elijah the Prophet who would occasionally visit them. It was in this cave that R. Shimon stayed, studied the mysteries of the universe and composed the *Zohar* (which was later discovered by Moses de Leon). Near the cave, was a carob-tree whose fruit provided food. A spring of water inside the cave enabled them to wash and satisfy their thirst. That is how they lived a life of meditation for twelve years, until Elijah came to inform them of the Emperor's death and the cancellation of the decrees against them.

R. Shimon moved from the cave to Meron and there he died. Meron, thereby, gained ascendency over Peki'in and wore the crown of the Saint. It became the centre for mystics and all who sought the holiness of Bar Yohai. His grave became the site of pilgrimages and the Celebration. On Lag B'Omer night, the anniversary of his death, bonfires are lit which cast light far and wide and scatter sparks as far as Peki'in, even into the cave.

At first, Peki'in was very grieved and the celebrated cave was filled with sadness. Not that there was jealousy on the part of

Peki'in! Jealousy is not a good quality, but there was sorrow over the neglect of the cave and the few visitors to it.

Then something precious was done to make up for the loss. When it was decreed that Israel be exiled from the land, it was understood that Eretz Yisrael could not for one moment be completely without any Jews. After all, G-d had promised that He would not entirely eradicate everything. The fixing of the calendar depended on some settlement in Eretz Yisrael, as Maimonides pointed out in her *Sefer Hamitavot*.

When the decision had to be made regarding the permanent settlement, Peki'in was chosen. It had the privilege not granted to any other place in Eretz Yisrael; its children were not exiled nor ever uprooted from the holy soil. This privilege was granted for the sake of that holy man who used to say that G-d considered all the lands but did not find one worthy to give to Israel, except Eretz Yisrael. He had also said that whoever did not live in Eretz Yisrael was as one who had no G-d.

So, on the night of the Celebration at the grave of the Godly Teacher, Peki'in is praised and its glory sung.

THE FOUNTAIN OF RABBI SHIMON BAR YOHAI IN PEKI'IN

Situated in the Arab village of PEKI'IN, there is a well bearing the name, "THE FOUNTAIN OF RABBI SHIMON BAR YOHAI." To the hushed, almost noiseless flow of its waters, many medical cures are attributed. Credulous and pious people, of all sorts, as well as Kabbalists and mystics, come here to bathe in its crystal waters; while others come to drink thereof. The popular belief is that these waters possess the power of giving health to the sick, of fructifying the barren womb, as well an reinvigorating and rejuvenating the intellect that time or circumstance has dulled. Above all, the waters are endowed with the power to reveal the mysteries of Creation and the cryptic meaning of many biblical passages, such as the description of the "Chariot" in the first chapter of Ezekiel and the scriptural description of how the Universe came into being (Genesis I). These secrets, hidden from men in general, are revealed by Rabbi Shimon bar Johai in the ZOHAR, of which he is reputed to write in the care of Peki'in.

It is this fountain which is still known by the name of "The Fountain of Rabbi Shimon bar Yohai, to which miraculous cures and strengths are still attributed unto all who bathe therein or drink thereof.

Last year, the company which has made itself authoritatively responsible for the fresh water supply of Medinat Israel, MEKOROT by name, decided to stop-up this storied fountain and to convert it, instead, into a water reservoir for the surrounding fields, orchards and arable land. This move created much grief among mystics and Kabbalists, loyal to the memory of their saintly teacher. Most vociferous of all in his protest was Rabbi Zanwell. Telegrams of protest to the President, Prime Minister, Cabinet Ministers, Chief Rabbis, were dispatched by him in which he pleaded earnestly to prevent this outrage planned by MEKOROT. Happily to relate, he met with a successful response; and sincere efforts are now being made to effect a compromise which should please both sides.

When one of the water-engineers sarcastically plied Rabbi Zanwil with the question: "Do you wish to block our plan to supply water to the parched surroundings because of some foolish legends and questionable cures?" the bold reply was: "Folk-legends are not always, or necessarily, foolish!" Zaibeni continued: "This is tradition and not folk-legends and even I am ready to admit that it is not so much the legendary cures, which are attributed to its waters that have prompted me to take up the cudgels in my staunch defence for the preservation of the fountain. My main motive in my fight is on account of the traditional beliefs which cling to it." He then related to the engineer the tale unfolded to him by a venerable Kabbalist from Safed—the cradle of mysticism in the sixteenth century, while they both sat in the cave wherein Rabbi Shimon bar Yohai and his son, Rabbi Eleazar are reputed to have hidden during the thirteen years.

"The story he told me," continued Reb Zanwil, ran as follows: "The fountain in Peki'in was not created when the world was first called into being, but was created for the specific purpose of supplying water for the two fugitives—Rabbi Shimon and his son— during their hiding in the cave. When the prophet, Elijah, appeared one day before Rabbi Shimon announcing that Heaven was about to cause a fountain to appear at the entrance of the cave, Rabbi Shimon, at first, refused to avail himself to his wonderful gift. His reactions at Elijah's tidings were: "I do not deserve such heavenly care and provision. Moreover, it is not right for frail, mortal beings to trouble Providence to cater for their own private needs." When

he persisted in his refusal to avail himself o this miraculous intervention on his behalf, Elijah persuaded him that the fountain was
not specifically created for him and his son alone, but for all such
Jews who will categorically refuse to abandon or desert Peki'in
until such time when the Messianic Age will dawn, bringing Salvation to the entire world and resurrecting our glorious Dead.

"When the Rabbi Shimon heard this explanation, he agreed to
draw from the translucent, limpid waters, advising all those who
will faithfully cling to the soil of Peki'in to drink from this sweet
flow.

"It is for this reason, above all others," concluded Reb Zanwil
"that Jews ought never to abandon Peki'in entirely; especially
never to allow the fountain to be stopped-up."

A story like this they tell about the carob-tree. In the beginning divine protection caused a palm-tree to grow near the cave
with luscious dates to still their hunger. But Rabbi Shimon refused
to eat the dates. "It is not right for frail, mortal beings to trouble
Providence to cater for their personal needs. Providence changes
the palm-tree in a carob tree that grows everywhere and even for
animals. That the Lord has as a creature to nourish.

R. Mosheh Isserles

Meron influenced all parts of the Diaspora and crowds would
flock to the graves of holy men on Lag B'Omer, thereby associating
themselves in some way with R. Shimon bar Yohai and Lag
B'Omer at Meron. One of the pilgrimages was to the grave of R.
Mosheh Isserles, author of *The Mapah* [commentary on the
Shulhan Arukh], a pilgrimage which was associated with the one to
Meron and which gave expression to the longings for redemption
and the desire to be connected with Eretz Yisrael on this day.

Polish Jews used to go to Isserles' grave in Cracow on Lag
B'Omer. It was commonly held that he had died on this day when

he was thirty three [LAG] years old after composing thirty-three books. Even though scholars cannot verify this belief, it has been retained by the masses and has influenced the custom of visiting his grave. Reb Zanwil, a Polish Rabbi felt that the tradition should not be forgotten and decided to link it with the historic bond between the Diaspora and traditional life in Israel. It introduced therefore, into the Lag B'Omer program at Meron a memorial to Isserles, by way of lectures on his life and work. A few years ago, there was an exhibition dealing with R. Moshe Isserles; it included pictures of his synagogue in Cracow and his grave which was not disturbed by the Germans.

The fact that the Nazis left the tomb unharmed seems a miracle and many stories have been told. While remembering him at Meron, one of the elders told the following two stories:

The MAPAH and the SHULHAN

In the fifteenth century, R. Yaakov b. Asher wrote a monumental work of Jewish jurisprudence, *The Four Rows*. This book elicited notes and commentaries from the greatest scholars of successive generations. Among the foremost were R. Yosef Karo (who lived in Safed), author of *The House of Joseph [Bet Yosef]*, and R. Moshe Isserles (who lived in Cracow), author of *The Paths of Moshe (Darkhei Moshe)*. Seeing significance in the titles of these works, Isserles remarked that Karo had settled in Eretz Yisrael and thus had a house but he was still in the Diaspora and only had a path, not one but many, all of them paths of wandering.

At this point, the old man interrupted his story and told a tale about "The House and the Path," and then continued:

R. Moshe Isserles studied the opinions and decisions of the foremost Polish and German scholars and decided to write a new treatise that would provide a summary of all of Jewish law. Without telling a soul he set about the project. He went through all the sources, studied the decisions of all the sages who had preceded him, and then put the laws down on paper. This task was exhausting but he fought off weariness and worked throughout the nights.

More than four years he worked to compile a SHULHAN ARUKH calculated to weld and mould the entire Jewish people into a solid block of adherents to the Torah and the Jewish way of life. His aim was to unite all the various sections into a uniform group, all observing similar customs, all faithfully adhering to the categorical imperatives of the Torah. He knew that only in unity of faith lies strength; that creed must be wedded to deed. The authority he enjoyed, and the respect in which he was held by all and sundry—though even far removed from his native Cracow—inspired him to compile this standard code of Jewish Law.

Elated by his compilation, he was under the impression that he had achieved almost the impossible; and that his work would eventually become the *vade mecum* of every Jewish household. When he was about to launch his massive work before the public, he was apprised, one day, that another, the saintly Rabbi Joseph Karo, of Safed, had anticipated him by this work.

He had nearly completed his work when a visitor arrived from Safed. The very name "Safed" thrilled Isserles because he maintained contact with its sages and rabbis. Personally, he was not one of the mystics but he had great respect for them and was sympathetic to their teachings. This particular guest was most welcome, because he was obviously one of "the inner circle."

At the table, the visitor told his host the news of Safed and, after the meal, gave him a book. He said: "Thus far, you have honoured me with your prepared table [Shulhan Arukh]: now will I honour you with my *Prepared Table,* a new work composed by Rabbi Joseph Karo—a legal work from the heart of the world [I.E. the Holy Land] intended to bring all Jews to one table before the Lord." The visitor then related wonderful stories about the composition of the *Shulhan Arukh.* R. Yosef Karo would write during the night but Satan found out and commanded his messenger, the wicked ruler of the city, to forbid Jews to have lights in their homes at night. Naturally, Karo was extremely disturbed. The fireflies saw his distress and came in great numbers to his home to perch on the walls and on the table and thereby provided light for him.

When Rabbi Moshe heard this, his pulse quickened. He took the book, glanced through it quickly. The guest looked at him and noticed a mixture of joy and sorrow on his face. He understood the joy but could not comprehend the obvious sorrow. Isserles suddenly lifted his head, looked at the guest and asked: "Could you perhaps tell me who suggested to R. Yosef to write this *Shulhan Arukh?*" The visitor replied: "Who knows? I heard various versions in Safed. Some say it was the Mystic Voice *[maggid]*; others say that the idea was born in the brain of someone in the Diaspora and was transplanted in him by some mysterious divine way."

R. Moshe was thrilled by the second version and the odd phrase "the idea was transplanted in him." He asked: "Do you know what was the nature of this transplantation?" The visitor thereupon related marvelous secrets of the way the mind works and cited as an example an incident that occurred in Karo's Synagogue. Once, the master and his students came across a most difficult passage which they just could not explain. That night, Karo consulted his Mystic Voice and became full of joy (as Maimonides says: There is no joy like the removing of doubts). He impatiently awaited the morning when he would explain everything to his students. Morning came and the lesson began; Karo was in a wonderful mood anticipating the delight he would bring the disciples as they comprehended the passage. But an amazing thing happened. The first disciple began to read and immediately gave the correct explanation, the very same that Karo had heard from the Mystic Voice. He was astounded! How could the disciple have come upon it? Had he heard the Voice? At night, the Voice had told him that every idea, as long as it was hidden, was hidden from everyone; but once it was revealed to the world, it hovered in the air and could come to anyone, particularly to those who were attempting to grasp it. That is the secret of the "transplantation"; an idea is carried from one person to another. R. Moshe Isserles then understood that his idea had been carried over to R. Yosef Karo.

Isserles spent the entire night poring over the new book and comparing it with his son. At first, he noted the similarities, but closer inspection revealed differences, differences of customs practiced in different places, particularly between Sefardim and Ashkenazim. What was he to do now? Should he publish his book and ignore the *Shulhan Arukh* which followed the Sefardic practices? That would mean two distinct lawbooks for Jewry and could cause a split, Heaven forbid! Moreover, who had the right to make the final decision and where should it be made? There, in the house of R. Yosef in Eretz Yisrael or on the path, i.e. in the Diaspora?

R. Moshe wrestled all night with the question of one "table" versus two "tables." After all, in Jewish history there were always two: Rachel and Leah, Judah and Ephraim, Palestine and Babylonia, Spain and Germany; but the goal was always to make them one, as Ezekiel declared: "Behold, I take the tree of Joseph which is in Ephraim's hand . . . and I shall place the tree of Judah on it and I shall make them one tree, and they will be one in My hands . . . and I shall make them one people in the Land . . . they will not be two peoples any longer."

If there is to be but one tree, where should it stand? Should it be in Eretz Yisrael where there is a small group of Spanish exiles or here, in the Jerusalem of Poland, where most of the people unfortunately are?

R. Moshe finally concluded that the tree should rightly be there; the Tree of Life should be in the Land of Life, as Karo had written on the frontpiece of his book: 'It is a tree of life to all who hold fast to it.'

The REMA looked to his volume, his emotions were stirred and he gave way to grief, because he now felt that his own work had been eclipsed by the excellence of this codification. So many years of his hard research, he felt, had been wasted. This thought cast a shadow of sorrow on his face, hitherto illumined by the pride of achievement. Those who moved in his circle could not fathom the transformation of his moods and appearance. What had grieved their beloved Rabbi to such an extent? The REMA, however, kept his sorrow a close secret, locked in the innermost recesses of his heart.

What should he now do with his own massive Code? Should he publish it after all? If he did, what would the Jewish world think of having before it two Codes, both authoritative, both compiled by men who had wedded great learning to deep piety? This must not happen, he thought to himself, for Jewry would be perplexed at the possession of two Codes on the same theme—Judaism, as Creed and Deed. Perish the thought; this might lead to diversity, instead of uniformity, in life and practice. No! he came to the conclusion, this *impasse* must not happen. Accordingly, he decided not to publish his own Code.

No sooner did he decide on this action, when the thought troubled him that it might be unearthed one day, and published after his demise; and then what he dreaded would be implemented—two Codes! Should he burn his SHULHAN ARUKH? He soon dispelled this thought, however. How could he have the heart to burn a work which had taken him four long years, and at which he had worked ceaselessly, both day and night. For weeks on end, he was perturbed by the thought as to what was the best action he could take.

The Tree and the Grave

Having made the decision, Isserles paid no heed to all the

time and effort he had expended. He accepted the teaching of the sages: Just as one receives a reward for the search, so one is rewarded for ceasing. After all, he had not labored for personal glory; he had toiled for the sake of heaven. But what should be done with his manuscript? He was afraid to burn it and, besides, it was forbidden to burn words of Torah. To put it away? Someone might find it and decide to declare it an alternate Shulhan Arukh.

He was thinking day and night and could not sleep. One night, he was visited by a mysterious and fantastic dream. He found himself sitting in a Yeshivah in Heaven, where a most heated discussion raged regarding the legal procedure in a certain case. Opinions differed, and recourse was had to two Codes—one compiled by Karo, that was already published; the other, still in manuscript, written by the Rabbi of Cracow—namely, himself!

Pondering the significance of this visitation, he came to the conclusion that he must transmit his Code to heavenly authorities. He, therefore, decided to have his Code buried with him in his grave, so that it would accompany his soul heavenwards when death conquered life. From that day of the interment of his Code, onwards, he waited patiently for the time when he and his book would soar to Heaven, to be presented to the scholarly group of Gan Eden academicians.

The prayer of the REMA was that his decisions would not be against the real DIN. From that day he was looking for a grave for himself and for his code—four big volumes corresponding the four Turim.

He then happened to glance at the lone tree standing in the cemetery behind his house, a tree which no one knew when it was planted or by whom. The idea flashed through his mind to bury his manuscript there. A tree in a tree! Late at night, he took it and a spade and stealthily put them under his coat. He looked all around and seeing no one, he went out to the cemetery. A storm was raging outside and it tore open his coat, as if a hidden force was trying to grab the pages. R. Moshe grappled with the wind and, after digging a large hole under the tree, buried his writings.

Then he came to the burial society Hevra Kadisha of Cracow and asked them to sell him the grave with the tree. Imagine the surprise of those at the head of the *Hevra Kadisha* when they were faced with this request made by one still in the prime of his years; and yet already making provision, while still so young, for the time when a mere breath divides life from death! The head of the Burial Society—Rabbi Yitzhak by name—who, although he had already passed his four-score years, had not yet made provision in the event of his passing; yet this young Rabbi, barely thirty years old, was already reserving his final resting-place on earth! Amazement stared from the faces of those who headed the Cracow Burial Society, and they were puzzled at this strange request.

Rabbi Yitzhak spoke for the others when, taking his courage in both hands, he asked the young man: "Rabbi, why are you in such a hurry to think of the end? Surely, many years are ahead of you yet, before you need even consider when your days are no more."

To these questions, came the quiet reply of the REMA: "Rabbi Yitzhak, how do you know the length of our days on earth? Are we not advised to respect each day, lest it be our last? Should we not then ever be prepared lest tomorrow, or even this day, be our last?" This answer was made in a tone that was at once mystical as well as joyous; so that those to whom it was addressed had no alternative but to grant the REMA's request, namely, to reserve a grave for him in the old cemetery, not far from the synagogue in which he prayed and taught near to the strange tree.

The same legendary source goes on to tell us that on the very night following this strange transaction, the REMA silently made his way to the cemetery, where he dug a grave place for himself to be sure wherein he buried four massive volumes of his writings. Nobody knows his secret.

The only one who knew about this was the caretaker of the cemetery who had secretly followed the rabbi; before this caretaker died, he told his successor in great secrecy, so that he would protect the tree.

After Isserles had buried his book, he proceeded to compose notes to the *Shulhan Arukh,* adding the Ashkenazic practices and making a few corrections.

After some time, the same Palestinian Shadar visited again. He told him all that was going on in the Holy Land. They ate and talked; then R. Moshe turned to the guest and said: "Last time, you brought me as a gift from Eretz Yisrael *The Prepared Table;* now, I am giving you a gift in return, *The Tablecloth (Mapah)* which I have prepared for *The Table.* He presented him with his commentary to the *Shulhan Arukh* and asked him to give it to R. Yosef Karo and to tell him that *The Tablecloth* had been created before *The Table* but its measurements were taken afterwards.

The mystics who examined the book found in it many wonderful things and noticed allusions to questions which had bothered R. Moshe, particularly about differences in customs.

When R. Yosef received the *Mapah,* he understood all that had taken place and appreciated what his friend had done. He went and bought parchment for one hundred *dinars,* wrote on it a complete Torah and sent it to Isserles as a gift.

Ever since the burial of Isserles' book, the tree grew beautifully and its branches spread in all directions. No one understood the secret of its luxuriant growth. When the sprigs began to interfere with the passage between the grave, there were some who wanted to trim them. R. Moshe, however, stopped them and, before he died, he asked to be buried under that tree.

The tradition has it that he died on Lag B'Omer in 1572 and was buried on the same day under the tree. Since then, thousands annually visited his grave on Lag B'Omer. During the course of time, the two were joined and watched over each other, the grave over the tree and the tree over the grave.

It once happened, on Lag B'Omer, that the Burial Society wanted to cut the tree down because it bothered the throngs who came to the grave. But the Caretaker, who knew the secret, stopped them. Another time, some of those who came to the grave were scratched by the tree and, in their anger, wanted to remove it despite the protests of the Caretaker. All of a sudden, a heavy thunderstorm broke out and drove everyone away. This was taken as a sign from Heaven not to harm the tree and it was left standing.

When the Nazis entered Cracow and destroyed the Jewish Quarter, they went to the cemetery and desecrated all the graves. The tree then lowered its branches and covered R. Moshe's grave. The Nazis left the site untouched and the branches have remained hanging as if in mourning to this day.

When the Jews of Poland returned from Siberia and arrived in Cracow, they went to the cemetery right away. How amazed they were to see the tombstone of R. Moses Isserles standing among all those that had been overturned and desecrated and the tree shading it with its branches lowered downwards.

MEKOMOTH KEDOSHIM IN SAFED

In Safed, town of the Kabbalists, there are many ancient syna-gogues, the most noteworthy of which are:— *(2,1) The Synagogue of RABBI ISAAC ABUHAV (the Second), born 1433, exiled in the Expulsion from Spain. This synagogue possesses an antique Torah scroll, which used to be carried in procession to Meron on the eve of Lag Ba'omer. *The Synagogue of RABBI JOSEF THE BUILDER (Rabbi Banah), of the first generation of Amoraim. Rabbi Banah used to say: "For those who study the Torah for its own sake, it becomes a healing medicine" (Taanit 7a). He is said to have engaged in marking the graves of holy men and to have entered the Cave of Mahpelah (the burial place of the patriarchs) (Baba Batra, 58a). *(2,2) The Synagogue of the ARI (Rabbi Isaac Luria Ashkenazi), greatest of all Kabbalists, born in Jerusalem in 1534, died on 5 Av 1572.

THE H'ARI HAKADOSH

In the old city of Jerusalem near the synagogue of the Oz-Hachaim stands the house of the Ari Hakadosh Rabbi Yitzchak Lurie.

Over four hundred years ago, Rabbi Shlomoh Lurie lived in Jerusalem. He was a saint and a Hasid; and his wife was a very righteous woman. They lived together happily and contentedly; yet there was one problem which caused them worry—they were childless, a fact which gravely shadowed their lives. They used to distribute great amounts in charity and prayed to God that they might be blessed with a child.

In his later years, Rabbi Shlomoh had an extraordinary dream: There appeared before him a heavenly visitant, who said, "I am the Prophet Eliyahu. You should know that your prayers were accepted when they reached God, blessed be He. In a year from now, you will have a son—one who will illuminate the world with his holiness and heavenly wisdom. When the time for his circumcision arrives, wait until you see me in the room in the identical form in which you see me now."

Rabbi Shlomoh related the dream to his wife. Both believed in it and waited patiently until what it had foretold came to pass and so it was. A year later, Rabbi Shlomoh's wife bore a son. When the eighth day arrived, Rabbi Shlomoh invited all the important people in the city of Jerusalem to the *Brith*. Everyone, together with the man who would perform the circumcision, left for the Synagogue where the ceremony would be performed.

Rabbi Shlomoh, himself, was the Sandek. All was in readiness and Rabbi Shlomoh was told to go and sit on the couch and hold the child for the circumcision; but the Rabbi was looking around the Synagogue for the arrival of the Prophet Eliyahu. He used all kinds of excuses to delay the ceremony a little while longer, as he had been instructed; he must wait for the Prophet before the *Brith* could be held. Finally, just in time, the Prophet Eliyahu did appear and stood right next to Rabbi Shlomoh. Now it was he who said: "Go and sit on the couch and take the child on your lap." The Rabbi did as he was bidden. He went to the couch and sat down; and it was then that an extraordinary thing occurred: The Prophet Eliyahu himself sat down on the lap of Rabbi Shlomoh, took the child out of the hands of the *Sandek* and placed it upon his own knees. It was in this manner that the child was circumcised. No one saw the Prophet; all were sure that the father had held his son during the ceremony. The child was named YITZCHAK. After the *Brith,* the Prophet Eliyahu told Rabbi Shlomoh: "Take your child into your hands and know how to appreciate him, because he will be a great and holy light to the world!"

The first years of Yitzchak's childhood passed. It was easy for all to see that he was growing into a genius. With each teacher who taught him, he could not remain for more than a few months because he so soon outgrew all the students in their studies. While still in his ninth year, Yitzchak knew the Bible and *Shas* and *Posekim.* All the great men of Jerusalem were amazed at the child's wisdom and shrewdness and the most learned men in the City would spend their time with the young child studying Torah—considering him an equal in knowledge.

The father clearly remembered the words of warning of the Prophet Eliyahu and watched over his child as the apple of his eye, supplying him with all that he needed and teaching him how to lead a life of holiness and purity, so that he would grow into a holy person. This, however, was not for long. When the boy reached his tenth birthday, Rabbi Shlomoh suddenly passed away. The loss of all his fortune had broken his heart and Yitzchak became a poor orphan in the hands of his lonely mother.

The rich people in Jerusalem offered to take care of her and her son in the way to which she was accustomed; but the pious mother refused to take advantage of their offer. She would not live on charity and preferred to do her best to provide for herself and her child. A short time later, the mother judged it wise to confide in her son. "My dear Yitzchekel," she said softly: "We are now extremely poor and above all, I am also weak and sick. I have no strength to work any more and I cannot take money from others; moreover, I cannot take you away from your Torah studies just to help me. It is my plan, therefore, that you should leave for Alexandria, in Egypt. My brother, the rich Reb Mordechai Francis, lives there. He will support you and you will be able to continue and to study diligently. As for me, the Almighty will support a poor and lonely widow . . . ."

Before consenting to go to Alexandria, however, the boy consulted the Rabbis of the town. He was happy to receive their blessings—material as well as spiritual; but he could not restrain his tears when they blessed him for a long life and advanced old age. He seemed to have a premonition that he would soar to Heaven in the very prime of his life.

In due course, he arrived at his uncle's house where he was welcomed and assigned to his own private quarters—for it was a large house—where he could sit and study without being disturbed; but he was always to eat at the family table and be treated in all things as though he were his uncle's son. His uncle took Yitzchak to the Dean of the Yeshivah, to whom he also handed the sealed report from the Chief Rabbi of Jerusalem. When the Gaon, Rabbi Betzalel Askenazi, opened the letter and read it, he trembled with excitement. He stood up immediately, in honour of the child, and began to converse with him on Torah thoughts.

The *Rosh Hayeshivah* was astounded at the genius of the boy. Calling the uncle aside, he said: "What is written in this letter, does not describe the boy even by half! You must know that this child is a Heavenly Light in the world and it is the greatest merit for you to have Yitzchak in your house." Hearing these words, the uncle embraced and kissed the boy and cried for great joy. He supplied him with all his material needs and held him in great honour.

Yitzchak learned with fervour and diligence, studying day and night with a most loving disposition. All who heard his sweet voice during the long winter nights, remained standing in spell-bound admiration. That he was a genius was certain and he could reply to many questions with a single answer. He opened the eyes of all who knew him to the hidden depths of the Torah.

In the meantime, Yitzchak's mother yearned for her son and the boy pleaded with his uncle that he might send a message to his mother inviting her to come to Alexandria. His uncle immediately complied and soon his sister was in Egypt and mother and son lived with Reb Mordechai, all the three blissfully contented together.

The years passed and Yitzchak was now fifteen years old. His uncle, Reb Mordechai, had a daughter of the same age. She was a most pleasing girl, having matured gracefully and she was also good and religious, possessing all the qualities essential for an excellent Jewish wife. The matchmakers often came running to the house suggesting all kinds of wonderful alliances for her; but Reb Mordechai realized that there was no better match than his sister's boy. When he spoke to his daughter about this, she readily agreed and said that although she knew him so well, since they were both living in the same house, she had never met anyone with so many excellent qualities. Mother and son also agreed to the match because they, too, recognized the great qualities of the young lady.

A short time later, the celebrated wedding took place. Not only were all the important people of Alexandria invited, but the poor also were made welcome. Directly after the wedding, Reb Mordechai, the happy father-in-law, built a house for the young couple on the shores of the river Nile, in the quarter known as "Old Egypt" where the air was good and healthy. He gave the couple a great deal of money so that they could live a full and happy life, privately and without disturbances from without.

Husband and wife together studied the Talmud and Commentaries and their studies were on a mutual high level. Together, they plumbed the depths of the Torah. It was at this time that Rabbi Betzalel Ashkenazi compiled his great work the *SHITAH MEKU-BETZET,* with the young Rabbi Yitzchak helping him in his labours.

After seven years, Rabbi Yitzchak began to study on his own, separated from the rest of the world—studies of *NISTAR,* that is, hidden studies. For eight years, he studied in this way with great steadfastness and holiness. He never spoke to anyone except words of Torah. Every Friday night, the young couple would visit their father-in-law's house and remain over Shabbat. During these Sabbaths, Mordechai's house was filled with Torah wisdom. The greatest Torah scholars of Egypt who were invited, welcomed the opportunities of discussing with Rabbi Yitzchak the most intricate passages of the Torah. He answered each one in brief sentences, directly to the point. Even his talks with his own family were never lengthy and always in the Holy Language.

When Rabbi Yitzchak attained the age of thirty-six, he went to Safed, in Medinat Israel, to join the esoteric circle of Kabbalists. For many months, he sat at the feet of the greatest of them all, the renowned Rabbi Moshe Cordovero, known as the "REMAK." When the latter departed this life, the Kabbalists turned to Rabbi Yitzchak, the *"ARI,"* as their leader. In contrast to the rest of the Kabbalists, he gave his mystic teachings publicly. In addition, he arranged for a special house in which he resided together with his selected disciples.

It was the practice of the ARI to tour the hills surrounding Safed, in the company of his disciples and to visit the holy sepulchres found in the local cemetery. On his walks, he would expound to his followers sublime and lofty thoughts and explain the mysteries of the Torah. Strangely enough, he committed none of his teachings to writing and even prohibited his disciples from doing so.

Even his youngest followers were renowned as scholars, possessing infinite knowledge both of revealed and cryptic learning. One of the most famous of these was Rabbi HAYIM VITAL. He it was who collected and systematically arranged the Torah according to the teachings of his celebrated Master. True to the ARI's wishes, Rabbi Hayim adamantly refused to publish the doctrines of the ARI; but his son, Rabbi Samuel Vital, did publish a book containing both the teachings of the ARI as well as those of his father. The method adopted by the ARI is based on the *ZOHAR* and founded on the well-known Kabbalistic hypotheses such as the Secret of the Ten Spheres, the Power of Limitation *(TSIMTSUM)* and the mysteries of the Transmigration of the Soul. To all these, he supplied a special, practical meaning, according to a combination of selected names.

In his House of Studies, many customs were crystalized and translated into observances that were founded on his way of life and on his system of imposing his doctrines. As a result, his teachings permeated Jewish communities the world over. Examples of these are the method of receiving the Shabbat at its approach; the observance of YOM KIPPUR KATON (on the eve of ROSH HODESH); the holding of the Midnight Vigil (in mourning for the Destruction of the Temple) and others, of a similar nature.

The ARI also composed special *ZMIROT* (Hymns), three of which were specially designed for Shabbat. These are the three beginning with, *"AZAMER BISHVAHIN"* ("I will Sing Praises . . ."); *"ASADER LISE'UDTA* ("I will Arrange for the Meal . . ."); and *BNEI HEICHLA* ("The Sons of the Temple"). These hymns have penetrated into most Jewish homes and are recited with tuneful, joyous melodies throughout far-flung Jewry.

It was also the regular custom of the ARI to seek solitary contemplation, alone with his disciples, in the vicinity of the graves of the Righteous and Pious who had winged their way heavenwards and to seek affinity and affiliation with their souls. He was the means of discovering and revealing many hallowed sites in Eretz-Israel. The holy ARI soon became a legendary figure, even while he still walked on earth, an image of holiness which was magnified when he left his followers mourning at his premature departure from their earthly circle.

In a short time, Rabbi Yitzchak became famous throughout the world as a Man of G-d. He became a Gaon both in open and in hidden studies. The greatest of the wise men among the Kabbalists would inquire of him as to matters of Kabbala which they were unable to understand but which he explained clearly to them. With one voice, all said that there was no one like him anywhere in the world; and soon they shortened his name to the "H'ARI HAKA-DOSH," which stood for the letters of *HARAV ALOKI RABEYNU YITZCHAK*. Soon, men came to him from all the known world to ask about questions of Law, or to beseech his blessings. All were welcomed with a friendly face and his advice was always wise and to the point. His blessings would materialize in the most fruitful way. Thousands of people were cured from illnesses through the blessings of the ARI HAKADOSH. Never accepting money for his services, he would often distribute it to the poor who came to him and he helped them when they were in trouble or distress. This wonderful kind of sympathy and understanding made him universally beloved by the thousands of people who surrounded and thronged to his house in order to obtain an opportunity to see him, speak with him and receive his advice and blessings.

Many are the legends both of an ethical and educational nature which the disciples of the ARI relate concerning him. They tell of his efforts to bring Redemption nearer and they even invested him with a special *aureole* of saintliness such as that which is associated with the "Son of Joseph, the Messiah," because he compelled them to repentance and to strive to usher in the Messianic Age. It is a fact that he instigated many to ascend to sublime heights and thus to bring Salvation nearer.

The fact that many followers of the Gaon of Wilna (the *GRA*) and the Hasidic school of the *BESHT* immigrated to Eretz-Israel, was sparked off by the methods followed by the ARI.

THE ARI

Actually, the *ARI* was not the founder of a cabbalistic method or approach, nor did he endeavour to explain his esoteric doctrines in the superficial manner followed by CORDOVERO. For the latter explained the ZOHAR by finding parallels from life and events around them. The *ARI,* however, uttered his teachings in a kind of sudden and spontaneous manner, seemingly unprepared, but cascading forth voluminously and voluptuously as if they were automatically triggered-forth, giving the impression that they were divine revelations issued from the lips of the *ARI.*

His utterances streamed forth eloquently, with NIAGARA-like fluidity. The remarkable fact was that each utterance comprised detailed concepts, all united into one harmonious teaching, although some of the links apparently seemed unconnected. It was his disciples, especially Rabbenu HAYIM VITAL, who categorised the utterances of the Master into FIFTY GATES AND SEVEN PALACES, assembling them all in a definite method which he had made his own. His peculiar method is prominently reflected in the scores of concepts and hundreds of explanations, as well as in his approach that was so different from that of his predecessors in many most fundamental teachings.

This divergence of opinion is great and important for students of *Cabbala* and mystics, generally. The limitations set by an article do not make it possible or desirous to draw attention to all these divergences; hence, will we suffice ourselves with pinpointing a few of those which project his singular personality and which are connected with his early origin and characteristics, especially with the method he employed in explaining the *ARI's* teachings to the ordinary reader.

The fundamental elements of the *ARI,* which he enlarged and to which he added a new touch, were the concepts of LIMITATION, BREAKING OF THE *MEDIA (KELIM),* the FIVE FACES and their relation to the TWO WORLDS. These FIVE FACES and their relationship to the human soul—which is also sub-divisioned into *five* categories, he called NUN—HAI, "THE SOUL OF THE LIVING SPIRIT *(YEHIDAH).*

It is difficult to explain these concepts within the confines of a brief essay, especially since they are inextricably interwoven with the very esoteric doctrines of the Godhead, with Creation itself, and with scores of other unrevealed ideas. We will endeavour, however, to explain them in so far as they are connected with his theory of correcting (TIKKUN) which, as we have already seen, seems to have been his main mission during his brief span of life.

The Concepts of LIMITATION (TSIMTSUM) and the "BREAKING OF *MEDIA*" (SH'VIRAT HA'KELIM), which for the basic teachings of the *ARI,* make it their aim to explain the *phenomena* of deficiencies in the world here below. They seek to shed light on the confusion of good and evil—a confusion which seems to be as old as Creation itself. It would seem as if the Creator, from the very first, instituted these deficiencies in order to provide man with a mission to repair the breaches whenever and wherever he encounters them.

Another fundamental concept, also intended to be corrected by man, is that of the "FIVE FACES," and the connection between them and the human soul. This fact also provides man with the possibility of effecting an improvement to his own soul. According to the doctrine of the *ARI,* which is also based on the *Cabbala,* all the different souls of man stem from one source and one period— that of the first Man. The ARI regarded ADAM as the most complete and perfect man; that is, before he sinned. In this first man (ADAM HA'KADMON), were planted various degrees of potentialities; in his many limbs and arteries, were fixed the connecting-links between the divine soul and the FACES that nobly reflect the spiritual bounty inherent in the human soul.

When Adam sinned by eating of the 'Tree of Knowledge,' he caused the sin of sending-forth a battle-array of forces inimical to the realm of the spirit. The result was that these select souls became intermingled with the unworthy souls and *vice versa*. It is for this reason, that to every individual soul there clings something which is alien to it; it is this alien appendage which is called *KLIP-PAH* (PEEL) and is the evil part in man which he must endeavour to repair, so as to purify his heavenly soul of base "peels" and "shells" (KLIPPOT).

These revelations can appear to a man by *three* paths. The first is by the STUDY OF THE TORAH; this means, that the trinity of the SHECHINAH, ISRAEL and THE TORAH must become merged into *one*. It is the "blue-prints" drawn up in the Torah which the Divine Architect of the Universe consulted when He brought the world into being with his *"FIAT"*—"Let there be!" He also endowed each letter of the alphabet with the power, by means of permutations and combinations, of revealing secrets hidden from the visual sight of man. The Torah does not contain explicit secrets and hints; these are to be discovered in, and quarried from, the rich mines of the ZOHAR and other works of the mystics and Cabbalists.

According to the Cabbalists, from an intense study of the ZOHAR, wherein RABBAN SHIMON BAR YOHAI reveals many of these secrets, man will be able to effect such *TIKKUN* and to pace life with dignity and extreme piety. These secrets, found in the ZOHAR, were revealed to BAR YOHAI and his disciples only. When he died, these esoteric doctrines were transformed into secrets and were written down in a cryptic style. Only those who bury themselves in a deep study of the ZOHAR and plumb the very depths of its profound doctrines, will be able to uncover some of these invaluable mysteries of life and the soul. It was the saintly *ARI* who devoted such deep, concentrated and ceaseless study of the ZOHAR, tirelessly praying as he pored over its contents day and night: "O Lord, uncover my eyes that I may be able to look with breathless adoration at the wonders of Thy Torah." This fact has been handed down to posterity by his disciples and other saints. It was the various saints, especially Elijah the Prophet, who has been entrusted with the custodianship of these heavenly secrets, that has revealed these mysteries to the reputed author of the ZOHAR. At times, he was transported by Elijah to the Heavenly Temples (HECHALOT) of learning, there to sit at the feet of the Prophets and the TANNAIM, themselves.

It was by his intense, comprehensive study of the Creation, which reflects the Creator in all His handiwork and by a knowledge of the meaning of every letter of the Torah, that BAR YOHAI was enabled to hand down these divine secrets, hidden from ordinary men, to all those who make the ZOHAR their spiritual food and drink during every day of their life on earth.

It is by means of such absorbing contemplative study and in which body and soul cooperate, that man can exclaim with JOB: "From my flesh, I see God." It is from the bodily facets of man that, according to the Cabbalists, one can begin the better to understand the structure and purpose of the universe.

It is well-known that all the component parts which form the body of man are patterned on the heavenly "Image." Man is but a *shadow* of the Above which has assumed bodily, concrete shape during his tenure of earth. The human body is but a gloomy, impure bridge, containing within it the soul of man which is but a spark of the Heavenly Light and which never is separated from its divine source.

The Ari

These sources are most important and are linked with the parable cited by CORDOVERO, of the man who carries such a burden on his shoulders, that no accurate account can be given of its exact weight. Every estimation is hedged round with doubts and hypotheses of a speculative nature. It is only the one who carried the burden himself that can at all have an inkling of its exact weight.

After the Ottoman Empire had conquered Palestine, many saintly scholars who had hitherto resided in Turkey, among whom were many Cabbalists and others who had formed themselves into separate sects, united by their passionate belief that the Messianic Age was drawing night, and which they even claimed was discernible on the horizon, came to take up residence in SAFED. It was this holy city, nestling mysteriously among the majestic hills from many of which glimpses of lovely Lake KINNERET below could be obtained, which became the place beloved of the mystics and the home of the Cabbalists, especially in the sixteenth century C.E. It was here that they instituted prayers on special occasions, apart from the three daily statutory prayers; and it was here that the midnight vigil *(HATZOT)* first became the practice of those who prayed for the Redemption and "the gathering of the exiles" (KIBBUTZ GALUYOT)

The throngs who prostrated themselves at the graves of the holy also aspired thereby to catch some of the "divine sparks" and the revelation of secrets which might be triggered-off from these venues of the glorious departed. It was this wish that was expressed by the *ARI* himself when he visited the sepulchre of R. SHIMON BAR YOHAI.

THE SPIRITUAL SPARK
OF MOSHE RABBENU

The year 5732 commemorates the four-hundredth anniversary of the passing of the saintly ARI which occurred on the 5th of Ab, 5372. To celebrate this event, Rabbi Zanwill was arranging a whole series of conferences, lectures and seminars in order to popularize among the wide public his cabbalistic doctrines and mystical approach to Judaism. In addition, he is compiling and diffusing characteristic, esoteric legends which the years have woven around the life and thought of the *ARI*.

Cabbalists firmly maintain that, within the ARI, a spark of the soul of MOSHE RABBENU glowed brightly. Though based on somewhat shaky foundations, mystics refuse to be shaken in this belief. One of the arguments which they advance in corroboration, is that just as Moses spent his early years in Egypt, so did the ARI. Moreover, it was the latter who brought to light the mysteries inherent in the Torah, thus completing the doctrines which Moses brought down from Sinai's firecapped and thunderous peaks during the Revelation.

In his own characteristic manner, Rabbi Zanwill elaborates this fantastic legend with the support of an ancient tradition which was once narrated to him by an aged Cabalist of Safed. It tells the curious, visionary story of the birth of the ARI, and has its source in Jerusalem.

One night, when the winter cold and rain enveloped Jerusalem, its residents retired early to sleep. Among these was one, Rabbi Shlomo by name. His wife, who was in the last stages of her pregnancy, did not feel very well that night. This was another reason for their early retirement, so as to gain refreshing sleep. In order not to disturb his wife's sleep, Rabbi Shlomo decided to curtain his evening prayers and studies and follow her example by calling the early hours of night a day completed.

Imagine his surprise, when midnight brought a heavy knocking at the door. His first reaction was distressed alarm. Who could it be that sought admittance at such an unearthly hour and on such a wretched, tempestuous night? Approaching the door which led to the street, he enquired cautiously: "Who is there?" The reply he received was: "It is a Jew, homeless and dejected, who is seeking a night's shelter at this miserable time. I can no longer endure the biting gusts of wind and the tempestuous rain; so, please, let me in!"

Hearing this, Rabbi Shlomo immediately invited him in and greeted him with traditional Jewish hospitality, saying: "By all means come in and regard my house as your home for the night. Tell me, however, what made you knock at *my* door among all the other houses in this dark alley and in this most hidden quarter of the town wherein my house is situated?"

The reply of the strange, casual wanderer was simple and surprising: "Seeing that every house in the city was plunged in darkness, I came to the conclusion that everyone had gone to sleep for the night and I was hesitant to knock at the door of any of the houses lest this would alarm those therein. Imagine, therefore, my joy when I perceived a light gleaming from one house and I thought to myself: "Here, at least, there is still somebody who is awake probably studying or celebrating his midnight vigil by reciting prayers for the re-building of the Temple, the glory which was once that of Israel in the Holy City."

This explanation by the unexpected visitor, worked much wonderment in the mind of Rabbi Shlomo. He mused to himself:

"How could he have observed a light shining from my windows when I had long since gone to sleep this night" (for the reasons above mentioned)? "So what sort of light did this visitor behold, beckoning to him from my windows?" These questions only passed through his mind without his framing them into words; but turning to the visitor, he exclaimed: "How could you have noticed a light shining from my house since I had retired for the night long ago?"

The visitor, however, was adamant in his statement: "Oh yes! I did see a bright light beckoning to me from this window," and he pointed to the room in which the Rabbi's pregnant wife was now firmly locked in the bonds of sleep. "But how could this be possible?" Rabbi Shlomo asked the intruder in open-eyed amazement, "Since the light of my wife's bedroom had been extinguished hours ago." Observing that his guest still clung firmly to his statement, Rabbi Shlomo quietly opened the door of the room in which his wife peacefully reposed in order to convince the other that he had been mistaken in imagining a light where none existed.

Indescribable, as well as unbelievable, was his amazement, however, when he beheld that his wife's bedroom was flooded with a light, unseen by mortal gaze both in earth and in heaven. Turning to the visitor, he gasped in astonishment: "What can this betoken?" The latter, whose face was now illumined with a similar light as that which filled the room, joyfully gave answer to his host's wonderment: "This light is none other than that which will shine from the soul of your son, now waiting to emerge from his mother's womb. The light which I first beheld from without and which we both now witness from within, is none other than the bright light with which your son will illumine the world when he is grown-up!"

The guest then continued his breath-taking announcement: "Rabbi Shlomo, surely you have not forgotten the legend surrounding the birth of MOSHE RABBENU which tells us that also when he was born, the room in which he first saw the light of day was, likewise, flooded with light. In your son, there will always glow that divine spark which suffused the whole life of our Lawgiver!"

The midnight intruder continued his marvellous tidings: "Your son will, in the course of time, illumine the whole world with the light of his esoteric and mystical doctrines. May I stipulate one request which I hope you will not refuse me? This is: to wait until I appear to you again before you effect the circumcision of this child who is about to be born."

On the eighth day, just when the circumcision was about to take place, this mysterious visitor reappeared in the nick of time!

What greater proof, argue Cabbalists, can there be than that the Divine Spark of MOSHE RABBENU illumined the soul of the saintly ARI?

THE CHILD THAT FLOATED IN THE AIR

It was custom is Jerusalem in order to educate the child in the ways of the Torah even while still in her womb, the mother would gather some moss that grew wild in between the stones of the Wall. This moss, she would soak in the waters of a well adjoining the Wall, and then drink thereof—not for her own good, but in order to symbolize that she wished her child to be morally and spiritually nurtured from heavenly sources. For popular tradition has it that the pure waters cascading from the well near the Wall, have their source in the four rivers which flow from the Garden of Eden.

The pregnant mother-to-be would remain hours on end at the wall, pressing her full body against the Stones, as if to effect a co-ordination between the instruction she was later to give her off-spring, and the Holy Wall which has the SHECHINAH (Divine Presence) as its aureole.

Rabbi Shlomo exercised the greatest possible care to keep vigil over the unborn child, and to protect it—and the mother—from any untoward circumstances. He would pray ceaselessly for its welfare, constantly observing all the precautions suggested by well-wishers. No scheme—be it either trifling or one which demanded maximum effort—was too much for him to fulfil, in order that no harm (G-d forbid!) befall the child about to be pit-chforked, helpless, from the mother's womb, an with no language but a cry. He decorated the house in general, and the room in which the newly-born arrival would first see the light of day, in particular, with olive-leaves plucked from the trees planted near the river Plau. These leaves were very fragrant, emitting a most pleasant odour. Upon the wall, above the bed where the mother lay in confinement, he hung an inscription, printed in very large square letters, with the words of the Psalmist, "May the Lord guard and protect you; may He be thy shade on thy right hand!"

So large were the letters of these words, that even the smallest of the demons, who lie in wait in the chamber in order to inflict harm on mother and babe, would be able to read them without any effort or undue visual strain. The imps simply would not dare to harm mother and child after these solemn warnings.

As if these precautions were not sufficient as prophylactics, Rabbi Shlomo would hang long, thick curtains around the room, so as to shield and conceal it and those therein from the dire effects of the "Evil Eye." This strict cautionary measure had a twofold purpose: both to protect the newly-born babe from any physical harm; as well as to safeguard its soul against the machinations of demons and evil sprites who constantly gnaw at the soul, attempting to nibble its heavenly lustre away by such human vices as pride, passions, and wicked thoughts, generally.

The birth of the child flooded the whole house with a great light. So delighted was Rabbi Shlomo, that he gave a small party in his house for a few select guests. He invited ten of his closest friends to study Torah. When they had completed their study, they drank a toast to the child and his parents and ate with great relish the delicious luscious cakes that had been specially baked for the event. The child was then weighed, and its equivalent in money was exchanged in kind for bread for the poor, oil for the kindling of the lamps in the synagogue, and alms for all those in need of charity.

Texts were hung on the walls, and verses endlessly chanted, in which the protection of G-d was sought against lurking evil spirits; and a silver chain and medal were suspended round the child's neck, as a further charm and amulet, which would serve as a shield against the devilish machinations of the demons. Until the eighth day, that of his circumcision, small school-children were brought into the room of the confinement, and instructed to keep on saying the SHEMA—the password of Judaism. A lamp was also kept burning day and night in the room, symbolic of the heavenly light which should illumine the whole life of the child, so that he would be enabled to pace the earth with dignity till the end of his days. "For the Commandment is a light; and the Torah spells brightness!" All who visited the child in the room, called out loudly, "Unto the Jews, there was light!"

The custom of kindling a light originated in the period of persecutions against Jewish practices, instituted by the wicked Roman King, Hadrian; who, amongst other prohibitions, forbade circumcision to take place. The light was kindled in the cellar where the ceremony was about to be performed surreptitiously, in order to attract Jewish passers-by to enter and thus form the religious quorum (of at least ten male adults) necessary for the occasion.

With the death of Hadrian, the decree lapsed, but the custom of kindling a light remained, outliving the oppressor. Does not Jewish history teach that Jews have always been enabled to stand at the grave of their persecutors? In the course of time, a new reason for the light was given; it was taken to symbolize that the child would grow up to be a light and joy to his parents, and all among whom he moved. It was further interpreted as a symbol of protection, and as a guiding-light throughout the life of the child. When the light was lighted in his room, it was accompanied by the prayer: "May it be His Will that a Heavenly Light should illumine thy way from the cradle to the grave!" that is, from this world below with all its vicissitudes and frustrations, to the Life to Come, where all is rest for evermore.

As the light was kindled for this child, his father, Solomon, smiled beatifically, for he knew what would happen at his BRIT (as we have seen above) and how the child would always be the object of Divine vigilance and protection. He smiled, but not a word escaped his lips; the secret was too holy to divulge. On the eve of the BRIT, extra vigil was kept over the child. Violent stormy winds lashed in fury without, and the mother felt instinctively that evil spirits were waiting for the opportunity to harm her beloved off-spring. Throughout that night, she stood at the entrance to the room with a Bible in her hand which would serve as a kind of protecting weapon against approaching demons. At the child's head, as he was lying peacefully asleep, she placed a PENTATEUCH, and sprinkled the wholesome scent of rosewater round his cradle. Rabbi Shlomo, himself, hurriedly ran to the Synagogue, known as that of "Elijah the Prophet," wherein he regularly prayed. When he arrived there, he decorated the Chair (known as the "Chair of Elijah the Prophet") on which the Circumcision ceremony would take place, filled all the lamps with oil and spread coverings over the benches; as well as decorating the entire Synagogue with various flowers and sweetly-scented herbs. When dawn arose on the morning of the BRIT MILAH, Solomon betook himself to the MIKVEH (the Ritual Bath) so that he would usher his child into the Jewish fold in all purity. Disciples (called *GURI,* "young lions") of the ARI HA'KADOSH (The Holy Lion—the first letters of Aloki Rabbi Yitzhak, namely, Rabbi Yitzhak Luria) even go so far as to claim that he dipped the young babe with him in the MIKVEH!

On the morning of the eighth day, very early, Solomon took the child to the Wall, as our Patriarch, Abraham, did with his son, Isaac. Standing on the site of the Temple Mount, he raised the child on his shoulders and lifted him as high as he could. The idea then flashed across his mind to name the child Isaac, to be, like his biblical namesake, "an offering unto the Lord" as was Abraham's first-born of Sara. Solomon then brought the child to the Synagogue, where preparations for the BRIT MILAH (Circumcision) had previously been made by him. All was set and the stage was ready for the ceremony; but the most important guest—the SANDEK (Godfather)—who had promised to be in good time had so far not arrived. This puzzled those assembled and set them wondering as to the identity of the SANDEK. Why? Because popular tradition had it that Elijah, the Prophet, or the thirty-six anonymous Saints, on whose meritorious deeds the universe exists, and who are known by divers names, always turn up at the very last moment. Just when suspense is at its height and the twelfth hour has almost struck, they suddenly turn up, almost in the twinkling of an eye! This waiting for them to appear, creates a tension among those present; but this is a characteristic feature of these holy ones, and people can only possess themselves in patience waiting for their ultimate arrival.

In this instance too, the delay in the arrival of the SANDEK caused irritation and impatience among the guests, for the hours glided by, and the bright sun was replaced by lengthening shadows, and the day began to wane and make way for the evening. Though Rabbi Shlomo was constantly bombarded with questions as to who was the distinguished person for whom all had now waited for so long, he declined to divulge the secret his heart was nursing. Why should he reveal the name of him for whom all had long waited, when his answer might evoke jests and taunts? After all, not all present in the Synagogue were mystics, and adept in Kabbalistic lore. So of what avail would it be for him to disclose his closely-kept secret, enshrined for the present in the inmost recesses of his heart? No, he would wait; asking them also to abide patiently for a little longer yet.

Then something happened! Something so untoward and extraordinary that it created quite a mild alarm and consternation! As Elijah invisibly appeared and raised the child aloft, the cry arose, full of anxiety, from all lips: "THE CHILD WILL FALL!"

for little did they surmise that it was Elijah himself who was the SANDEK, and who was actually holding the babe firmly on his knees. How were they to know, since Elijah was invisible to the human eye? Their surprise was all the greater when they beheld the smile of contentment on the face of Rabbi Shlomo, when their own features betrayed only alarm. Little did they know that he was fully aware of the miracle, and was confident that no harm would befall the babe, about to be received into the "Covenant of Maraban."

He called to his guests: "Please, do not be alarmed! Thank G-d nothing harmful will befall my child. I can assure you that he will not fall to the ground; nor will anything disastrous happen to him."

Many are the legends told of the wonders surrounding that child who was suspended in mid-air during his circumcision. In the course of time, he was referred to as, "The joyous child who floated in mid-air!" for not even one of those present either saw, or suspected, that he had been firmly held during the process of circumcision, by none other than Elijah!

THE HOLY ZOHAR

One day, a man was sitting sadly in the synagogue, with a book in his hand; but he hardly seemed to be reading it. When prayers were over, the Rabbi, who had noticed the stranger, called him over and, with gentle kindness, questioned him about his prayer-book which, the Rabbi perceived was written with great supernatural and spiritual learning.

"Alas," said the newcomer, "I cannot tell you anything about my book. I am a Maranno—one of the Anussim—a Jew forced to become a convert to the Catholic Church in order to save my life; but still in mortal danger, if it be known that I have returned to the faith of my Fathers. I cannot understand what is in the book but, as everyone is using one, I also have one, lest I appear odd and strange."

The Rabbi took the man's book home with him, carefully examined it and compared it with the Holy Zohar and other sacred volumes. He studied it with devout prayer and fasting, so that his spirit might comprehend all its secrets. Such holy study brought to him the reward of a nightly dream, in which all that he had read was analysed and his judgments examined. At length, it was vouch-safed to him that although his studies were on the right path, many of the more profound meanings were being withheld from him. Only far more rigorous prayer, fasting and penance could bring him complete comprehension of the truths taught by Rabbi Simeon Bar Yohai.

Inflamed with a pure and holy desire to penetrate and under-stand the ultimate truths, the Rabbi greatly increased his already long hours of study and practised ever stricter spiritual and bodily subjecting. In time, his recompense was very great indeed. Instead of being visited by a dream, he was himself caught up in nocturnal visits to Heaven. There he was asked: "In which of the celestial yeshivot would he like to seek enlightenment? The heavenly Schools of the sainted Rabbis were all open to him;—that of Rabbi Akiba, of Rabbi Simeon Bar Yohai, of Rabbi Eliezer the Great? He was free to choose, and would be most warmly welcomes wherever he went.

Sometimes he preferred one, sometimes another. He had only to express a preference to be led immediately to that source of wisdom. Very many were the precious and secret truths vouchsafed to him. Greatest boon of all, he found that with each new day, having returned to his earthly environment, all that his mind had stored was crystal-clear and that he had a never-failing spring of inspired knowledge to pass on to his band of followers.

THE WELL CONNECTING
JERUSALEM WITH SAFED

According to mystic legend, a subterranean spring cascades its sparkling waters from Jerusalem to Safed, threading its labyrinthine course from Gihon across deep rivers, hills and dales, through caves and graves, until it arrives at Ein-Zetim at the entrance to Safed. According to the same legend, it was this trail that was followed by the saintly ARI when he left Jerusalem to take up his abode in Safed.

Though the ARI was born in Jerusalem, he had lived in Egypt since the age of eight. After he had reached his thirtieth birthday—over 400 years ago, he had a message from Heaven telling him to leave Egypt and depart to Eretz-Israel, for only thus could he rise to the spiritual heights designed for him. For have not the Talmudic Rabbis assured us that: "The very air of Eretz-Israel makes one wise?"

Acting on this divine admonition, he packed his few and scant belongings and made his way to Safed—the cradle of Mysticism. During the two years of his residence there, he developed his mystical interpretation of the words of the Torah, teachings which reverberated throughout the cabbalistic world.

The question which long remained unanswered was: "Why did he not make his way to Jerusalem where he had first seen the light of day when he emerged from his mother's womb? Why Safed, instead of the Holy City from which the Torah was first given to the world?"

To this problem, legend again had a ready answer. In fact, the ARI did blaze his trail from Egypt to Jerusalem; but when he arrived there in the early hours of the morning, long before the sunrise had painted the Judean hills with a riot of lovely colour, he had found the numerous gates of that walled city all strongly barred and locked, making admittance impossible.

His wonder grew apace at thus being unable to gain entrance to his birthplace. As he stood pondering what steps he should now take, a heavenly visitor appeared before him explaining the mystery of the locked gates which faced him.

Addressing the ARI, the heavenly visitor said: "Why are you so baffled at not being able to enter Jerusalem at once? Do you expect to be allowed therein while the dust and impurities of Egypt still cling to you? The Holy City cannot allow such paganism to defile its sacred places and make its air impure! You must first receive sanctification in its sacred waters and be hallowed by the pure air breathed forth by the hills of Judea, for only then will entrance to Jerusalem be possible. My advice," continued his heavenly visitor, "is to bathe in Gihon."

It was then that the ARI decided to bathe in the pellucid waters of the river Gihon and follow its winding course to whithersoever it might lead him. After much wandering and following the river's course, the ARI arrived at Ein-Zetim, the gateway to Safed.

It was a few hours before the arrival of the Shabbat that he came to Safed and his first point of contact was the grave of the Tanna Rabbi Judah bar Ilai. Emerging from his grave, the entombed Tanna called upon all to approach and hail the arrival of Queen Shabbat. The ARI immediately joined this winding procession. From that day, to his last on earth, he used to climb the hills surrounding Safed to welcome the arrival of Shabbat, accompanied by the souls of all the righteous and glorious Dead.

PRAISES OF THE ARI

There are those who believe in Reincarnation ; and the expiation of former sins in subsequent lives. The great ARI had a shrewd little tale to tell to his band of followers!

One day, a man whose affairs called him to travel overseas, came to the ARI and begged from him not only a blessing but, if possible, some indication of how his fortunes would—or would not—prosper. The ARI was heartening and reassuring, foretelling two great sources of happiness for the young man: He would meet, woo and marry a lovely girl, of great charm; and he would also come in for a pleasant sum of money. So, the traveller set forth, quite delighted at his prospects.

But the ARI construed for his followers, the pledges of good fortune which he had given: "This young man," he said, "once had a great friend, who caused him much pain and suffering. Through this false confidant, he fell into enemy hands, was taken prisoner, and only escaped from slavery some months later, after a large sum had been paid for his release.

"Now, however, this treacherous friend has been sent back in a new life, to make reparation to the young man whom he betrayed. For this reparation, however, he will come and live his new life as a woman, beautiful and kind; and it is she whom the young man will marry. They will be blissfully contented together for just the same number of months as the months of his slavery; then the wife will die; but the fortune she leaves her husband will correspond exactly to that sum which had to be paid for his ransom."

"But," said the followers of the ARI, "Supposing you had told this young man all the hidden meaning of your prophecy?

Would he not have had a chance to make a change in his plans—possibly in the course of his whole life?"

"It would have made no difference," said the ARI. "That which is ordained above, must come about. Somehow, at some time, all would have happened exactly as I have predicted." And, in due course, all that had been foreseen by the ARI, came to pass.

Soon after dawn, one morning, an Elder of Safed looked out from his house, and observed one of his neighbours, a woman still possessed of beauty and charm, go out from her door at this strangely early hour. The Elder was much disturbed in his mind, for he had lately been elected one of ten of the city's notables, who had been formed into a vigilance council to deal with and, better still, to forestall, evil deeds and bad behaviour.

Considering it his duty, the Elder slipped from his house and followed the woman, who turned into the precincts of a house, frequented by a man of doubtful character. Greatly upset—but nevertheless, somewhat self-important—the Elder continued his usual practice of early attendance at the Synagogue, and, after the Prayers, set about getting the nine other councillors together, to confer with them about what he had seen. Just as he was about to embark, rather unctuously, on his story, the Holy ARI cut him short before a word could be uttered.

Speaking as one to whom secret matters were revealed, the ARI bade the elder put all suspicions of the woman out of his mind, and speak no uncharitable word against her; for she was innocent of any wrong-doing. A passing traveller, temporarily seeking anight's shelter in the dubious house, knew the husband of this woman, and had brought from him, in the far place where he had sought work, tokens and pledges to the wife. On hearing of the arrival of this messenger, the woman had requested that he would come to her, or send to her whatever he might be bringing from her husband. Not so, the messenger had replied, he must go on his way, and yet had for her an important communication from her husband, which could be spoken into her ear alone. It was in this way, that the woman had been constrained to pay such an early call, in order to comply, faithfully and virtuously, with her husband's instructions.

The Elder was much taken aback; but went silently away, and made full inquiries into the whole matter. When he found that the ARI was right in every particular, he was greatly abashed and humiliated. Returning to the ARI, the Elder admitted that he had been mistaken in his suspicions; and asked for forgiveness.

The ARI, however, rebuked him: "It is to this woman that you owe sorrow and repentance, for your unjust thoughts of her. You have done me no wrong. Go to her, and ask forgiveness, and make your reparation to her!"

And so, the Elder learned true humility and charity; and all wondered and rejoiced at the holy insight of the ARI, into the hearts and minds of men and women.

Rabbi Isaac Luria, a most saintly and learned sage of Safed, blessed with supernatural gifts of prophecy and second-sight, was called by his followers, in deep reverence and affection, the "ARI." Not only was he wonderfully wise, but he had a heart of very practical love and helpfulness for all his fellow-men.

One day, there came to the ARI, a father deeply worried about his son, for the lad was delicate and although a persevering student, his approaching manhood seemed to bring him no increase in health and strength. The doctors looked grave, and prescribed this and that; but there was no lasting improvement, and he continued to have the same distressing pains.

The ARI told the father that no human remedies could cure the boy because of his sickness for the last ten years was due to his possession by an evil Spirit; and, as the poor man was naturally very reluctant to believe this, the ARI put the matter to a simple test.

Calling on the Spirit to answer, he wished to know why this poor student, in particular had been singled out as the victim of such possession? The Spirit told its resentful tale to the ARI and the father of the lad: "This boy," it said, "Young though he is now, was, in a former life, an elderly and influential citizen; and had a great deal to do with the administering of funds for the relief of the poor. I was one of those poor; and this man harshly refused to help me, and made no effort to look into my truly desperate circumstances. As a direct result of his cruel neglect, I eventually died of want, and cold, and misery. Now, by his own physical weakness, he is, in a new life, expiating his former sin; but I shall bring about his death, as surely as he brought about mine!"

Long and earnestly did the ARI argue and persuade—and, indeed, even bargain—with the Spirit for the life and health of the young man. In the end, the Spirit agreed to release the boy from the bondage of its possession; but on one condition—a seemingly perverse and foolish one, though not without sinister undertones: If, during the following three days, the young student spoke to a woman, or even saw her face, then the Spirit would reclaim him for its own, and bring about his immediate death. And, with this ultimatum, it went away.

Great precautions were taken to shield the lad from any chance encounter with a woman; and a different guardian was set over him for every hour of the next three days. Once, however, it happened that the Rabbi keeping watch, was suddenly called away, and hastily bade another take his place. This other, not realizing the importance of his trust, also, after a time went away. While the young man was thus left to himself, his mother and aunt happened to pass by his window and, seeing him alone, went in for a moment, to kiss him tenderly and ask how he was getting on . . . .

And instantly, the Spirit re-took possession.

It was well known among the followers of the ARI that he possessed supernatural gifts of divination, and could read the hearts and minds of men.

One day, a man—much troubled and perplexed by questions of conscience—came to the ARI, and asked him to read his heart. "If you will do this, and tell me what I should do," said the man, "I will listen, and pay heed, to your counsel; otherwise I shall go away and not trouble myself with these matters any more."

Then the ARI told him all the things that ever he had done; and the man was astounded at the accuracy of the ARI's knowledge. With shame and sorrow, he acknowledged his many faults and sins. On one point only was he adamant in refusing to concede the truth of what the ARI said. The matter in question was that this man had committed fornication with a woman working in his house. Flatly he refuted the charge. But the ARI, calling on the strange powers he possessed, caused the woman to appear before the man and confront him.

Then, at last, in an excess of guilty fear, the man confessed everything, moaning and groaning over his past evil life, and begging the ARI to obtain forgiveness for him, and to wipe out the vision of the woman from before his eyes. But, "Not so!" said the Rabbi, "For when a Jew commits fornication with a woman, he becomes as bound to her as are two copulating animals, and can never be free from her again—or only by dint of the most terrible mortifications and scourgings of body and spirit."

"Anything! anything!" cried the man, "So that I may win for myself pardon and Salvation in the next world!" "Even," asked the ARI, "one of the four ways of death prescribed by Jewish Law?" "Even so!" cried the poor wretch, "Be it by fire, by the rope, by stoning, or by the sword—so that my soul be set free."

Then said the Rabbi, wood must be gathered for his burning, as Fire must be his cleansing fate; so the man, who was rich, went on this errand and bought the faggots; then he was told there was yet a harder condition, for Fire was not enough; molten lead was demanded for sins such as his had been. So the rich man went and bought lead for the melting. At last, all was prepared, and the ARI bade the sinner lie spreadeagled on the ground, with his face turned up to the sky; then, to close his eyes, and open his mouth to receive the hideous purge . . . . But the ARI was, of all things, a merciful man; and his insight showed him that the soul of this man was so scoured by fear and remorse, and, indeed true penitence, that into that pitiful open mouth, turned up to him, he dropped not the ghastly hissing lead, but sugared confits such as children love; and, raising the poor sinner up in his tender arms, he blessed him, with assurances of heavenly pardon; and gave him uplifting prayers and praises to be read and studied each day; and especially those from the Holy Zohar.

Then the man went away, cleansed and strengthened in his mind and soul. He returned to his family and, after continuing for many years as an exemplary husband and father, he died in Safed, at a ripe old age, and much respected by everyone.

Too much care can never be taken to ward off the malign influence of Demons, who are always on the watch to destroy human souls! One day, a group of boys, having been given a holiday, were playing games, running and jumping, on the hillside near Safed. When they sat down to rest, they noticed a most strange thing! A disembodied finger was flicking about in the air, right in front of their faces! "Help me to catch hold of it," rashly said one of the boys, "And I will stick my ring on it, and see what it does!" No sooner said than done; and then the finger suddenly disappeared, ring and all. As they went home, they were secretly rather troubled and could not quite laugh it off, but, boylike, they did not bother overmuch; and soon never gave it another thought.

Years went by, and one of the boys, now a man, was betrothed to a young girl as beautiful as she was good; and there was great happiness in both families. But on the wedding day, just as the marriage ceremony was about to begin, a strange and hideous woman rushed in, and claimed the young man as her own! For had he not pledged himself to her with his own ring? And there it was, still on her skinny finger, and sure enough his own name was inscribed on it! A dreadful scene took place; and the outraged father-in-law took the weeping bride away home, and all was amazement and lamentation. Only the dreadful stranger was left. But the ARI called the young man aside, naming the woman as a most cunning She-Devil, and urging him to let himself be rescued from her clutches. The young man agreed with passionate grati- tude, for he was horror-stricken at the terrible situation into which his boyish prank, of so long ago, had placed him.

So the ARI ordered that the She-Devil be brought to him, that he might deal with her; for she had disappeared and hidden until she could snatch her victim and bear him away. The Rabbi, how- ever, ordered a more thorough search; and threatened her with Anathema, and all her circle, if she did not instantly appear. Sud- denly she confronted him, demanding that the lad should marry her, or she would destroy both him and his bride! But the ARI rebuked her with the utmost severity and authority, for the evil designs whereby she intended to entrap the innocent young man; but, boldly and insolently, she defied all he said to her!

In the end, however, she was no match for the ARI. Causing a bill of divorce to be prepared, he threatened her with a great Curse from which she would have no escape, if she did not accept this as a final end to all her wickedness; and undertake never, in any way, to harm the young man, nor his bride, nor anyone or thing con- nected with them. Powerless to resist the great virtue of the holy ARI, the She-Devil abandoned her vile designs, and vanished to be seen no more.

All being thus happily remedied, the bride-to-be was restored by her father to her future husband; and the marriage ceremony was celebrated with great happiness and rejoicings.

WHY DOES THE DOG OF RABBI JOSEPH DILA REINA BARK?

For many years, legend was rife in Safed concerning the Kabbalist, RABBI JOSEPH DILA REINA, whom the Angel of Death snatched from life at the time that he was performing, together with his ten disciples, spells and incantations calculated to hasten the approach of the Redemption. Despite all his ceaseless and tireless efforts to usher in the Messianic Age, he failed in his aim. The eagerly awaited Redemption did not arrive.

Heaven forfend that Rabbi Joseph should be placed in the category of false Messiahs, for his intentions were of the noblest; and he was honoured with the title and rank of a Rabbi in Israel. Though his opponents reprimanded him, on the grounds that it is contrary to Jewish teachings to attempt to hasten the "end of days" prior to its destined time, but to await its arrival patiently with the aid of national repentance and a return to the ways of the Torah, yet he enjoyed their respect because of the sincerity of his convictions, for they realized that he aimed at the "awakening of Heaven" by the "awakening of earth"—to employ the terms of classical, mystic sources.

However, even those who preferred to bide their time for the dawn of the Messianic Age, availed themselves of the legends surrounding the life of Rabbi Joseph dila Reina, in order to curb the fanatical frenzy of those mystics who applied all sorts of incantations and spells wherewith they hoped to hasten the "end of days." The fear was expressed lest the latter may once again give birth to a succession of false Messiahs, on the model of Shabbetai Zwi and Joido Frank—perish the thought!

When the present writer recently visited Safed—in connection with the four-hundredth anniversary celebrations marking the death of the ARI—which he is organizing this year (5732) throughout Eretz-Israel, he was conducted by the superintendent of ARI's grave, Rabbi Sa'adin by name, (he recently passed away) to an old ruin. On arriving there, the latter declared that it was here that the ARI believed that Rabbi dila Reina, who fought so hard for the arrival of the Messiah, was laid to rest.

The writer of this article, who happens to be a Kohen, expressed his regrets for having been brought in such close proximity with a grave. Though some opine that the graves of the pious do not defile, yet doubts passed through the writer's mind in this case whether this leniency applied here, in view of the diverse opinions held in connection with the *bona fides* of Rabbi dila Reina. Turning to Rabbi Sa'adin, the writer asked him, "Was it right of you to bring me, a Kohen, to this grave?"

Rabbi Sa'adin replied with a chuckle, "Yes, you need not have the slightest scruple in entering—for two reasons: one, Rabbi Joseph dila Reina is reputed to have been a saint; two, this is not actually where he himself was buried, but where his reincarnated being, in the shape of a dog, was interred. This dog persistently barked during the residence of the saintly ARI in Safed." Rabbi Sa'adin then unfolded an uncanny story which explained how the ARI revealed the reincarnated form of Rabbi Joseph dila Reina in the shape of a dog, which barked so loudly at all times.

The story ran as follows: "When the ARI lived in Safed, four hundred years ago (5732), a fierce black dog used to race along the streets each night, alarming all those who heard its wild, frightening howls. The dog used to bark frantically at all passers-by in the dark, narrow and labyrinthine alleys; and women and children were afraid to venture out at night lest they were molested by this dog's unwelcome attentions. The inhabitants lived under a constant fear, and the Rabbis sought all ways and means whereby to counteract this menacing intruder. Rabbi Rayim Vibal even composed a prayer to be uttered when confronted by the dog; but all to no avail. Not only did the dog persist in his barking, but, from bad to worse, it even grew wilder and more frightening as night succeeded night. Fright itself, however, is not actually a slayer of persons, and in the course of time people got acclimatized to this alarming nightly visitation—as they can do to the other unpleasant things with which existence abounds.

"When the saintly ARI first came to Safed, he was *incognito,* that is, nobody knew his real identity. Accordingly, he went about his ways unrecognized by those in whose midst he lived and moved. It was only the dog who sensed his arrival as soon as the ARI made his first steps in Safed; and it followed him all the way to EIN-ZEITIM, setting up a wild and frantic baying all the way. During the ARI's stay in the city, the dog persistently followed him, plaguing him with its wild bark at every step, and keeping up its vociferous din outside ARI's house both by day and night.

"The ARI was much intrigued to fathom the unwelcome attentions of this infuriated animal, which "dogged" his footsteps wherever he went! One day," continued Rabbi Sa'adin, "he followed the dog to this ruin where we are both now standing, and decided to 'have it out' with him. It should be mentioned that the ARI understood all languages, including those of birds and animals. Seizing hold of the ears of the dog, the ARI asked, "Dog! who are you really? And why have you not stopped barking, and following me, since my arrival here? What do you wish to achieve by your yelling?" The dog replied with a howl, wilder and more frantic than ever, which the ARI interpreted to mean: "I bark at you, and at all those who live here! I want them always to hear my clamour."

The dog then revealed, "I am the reincarnation of Rabbi Joseph dila Reina, who tried so hard in his life-time to usher in the Redemption, and yet failed so miserably that his soul was transplanted into me—a howling dog!"

Rabbi Sa'adin continued to unfold this weary tale of woe. "There are those who think—but incorrectly—that is was Satan himself who effected this reincarnation. No! It was Rabbi Joseph dila Reina himself who, after his death, asked to be transformed into a barking dog! Why? Because he laboured under the belief that only the ceaseless, wild noise of a mad dog might be effective in ushering in the dawn of Salvation.

The dog again took up his tale, "People eventually got used to my barking however, and, apart from evincing some alarm, soon took my unwelcome attentions in their stride, treating me as they did other pests and evils in life. True, they are still frightened by my barks, but they have got used to being frightened! My clamour passes over them as water from a duck's back. It is for this reason that I am tireless in following *you* with my uproar. You, who also are most desirous of ushering in the Redemption, know above all others: that the Messiah will come down from Heaven to earth, when he is preceded by the wild barking of ferocious mad dogs.

"When the ARI heard the voice of Rabbi Joseph dila Reina uttered by the dog (his reincarnation) he understood. Going home, he prayed, in a voice which sought to imitate the barking of the dog, thus: 'Save my soul from the sword and from the bite of a dog.' He also introduced into his Shabbat poem, which yearned for the Redemption, the barking of a dog. When the shadows lengthened, as the Shabbat day drew to a close, and the evening stars began to kindle in the darkling sky, the ARI sang his song—that was tinged with joy and grief; freedom and bondage. From his heart there were welled forth sighs, and the incurable hope that the ceaseless howls of the dogs which surround the Jew, all over the face of the earth wherein he finds a temporary and uncertain asylum, will one day succeed in raising earth to Heaven—when Death itself will die—and when Life will become an eternal song of Salvation."

THE MYRTLE

He was going out and singing as he held two branches of myrtles and told his disciples the meaning of the myrtles.

It is told of R. SHIMON b. YOHAI and his son R. ELAZAR that they once espied at the entry of Shabbat an old man carrying two small bundles of myrtle. It was almost sunset and they asked the man: "Tell us, why the myrtles and why all this hurry?" His laconic terse reply was: "So as to honour the approach of Shabbat." (*Sabb.* 33a) By way of explanation of this incident, he told them the story of Satan at the time of the Creation of the universe.

When G-d finished the Creation of the even of Shabbat, He had intended that only goodness should rule in the hearts of all things He had formed to pulsate with life on earth. He "sweetened counsel" with the souls of the righteous that would one day be clothed in bodies and descend as mortals on earth, as to the best way to ensure that only goodness would prevail on earth and cruelty and evil be totally unknown.

Many were the suggestions made at the momentous "Council Meeting," and opinions diverged. One suggestion was that man be endowed with "a good heart," while another opined that the remedy was "a good neighbour." Still others staked a claim for "a good eye" could ensure that goodness that goodness reigned supreme.

God agreed with the latter view, as did R. JOHANAN b. ZAKKAI (in Mishnah *ABOT*); accordingly, He created the universe in the shape of "a good eye." His intention was that Jerusalem should be "The City of Peace," and that the Temple should be the source and generator of Light. According to Jewish legend, He created them all in the shape of "a good eye." Thus we find in the Midrash (Gen. R. 63) in the name of R. SHMUEL HA'KATAN, the observation that "the world resembles the ball of the eye," in that the white thereof reflects the oceans which encompass the entire universe; while the dark pupil of the eye is symbolic of the world. The wrinkle in the pupil of the eye represents Jerusalem and the Temple therein.

G-d chose the myrtle to symbolize the eye, as it does in the Four Species *(ARBA MINIM)* used on Sukkot? when the LULAV symbolizes the spinal cord, the Willows, the lips, the ETROG—the heart, and the Myrtle—the eye (TANHUMA, EMOR).

When man takes a wife in marriage and builds a house—an act equated to the Creation of the universe, it is the traditional custom to go to meet the bride with a trig of the myrtle, so as to remind her of the Creation which was founded in the shape of "a good eye."

When Satan beheld the world dwelling in peace and filled with the sweet, aromatic fragrance of the myrtle, he became filled with jealousy. He cast an arrow into the world in order to arouse jealousy and hatred so that the eye of man be transformed from a source of goodness to the seat of all evil. His diabolical aim was to destroy mankind from the world's area by flooding them with the tempestuous waves of jealousy and by assailing those on earth with internecine warfare and brother strife. Satan did, indeed, perform wild things until the advent of Queen Shabbat, a day created for fragrant rest, both for master and slave, mistress and bondmaid; a day on which all are equal and all rewarded with rest; Yes, a day on which the eye of jealousy is bereft of all power. It is for this reason, that the myrtle was used on the Shabbat for its outer resemblance to the eye, as if to imply: "Guard over that good eye of yours."

Similarly, the myrtle became one of the fragrant symbols of the Sukkot Festival, because it is during this festival that the Jew is commanded to leave his luxurious home and take up temporary abode in the frail and haphazard festal booth. Thus this Sukkot festival likewise proclaims the concept of liberty, during which the "eye of jealousy" should be divested of all harmful deeds, and has co-opted the myrtle with the other three species to distil the fragrance of Jewish ceremonial and observance.

These "Four Species" correspond to the principal organs of the human frame—the heart, the lips, and the eyes, all of which must be welded into an harmonious orchestra performing the Will of our Heavenly Father. Is it not the intention of the Psalmist clear when he sang: "All my bones shall declare: 'O Lord, who is like unto Thee?'"

Suddenly, he turned to his faithful band and threw up his arms in an impassioned and joyous appeal to them. Ecstatically, he called on them that they should all come up to Jerusalem together with him; now, at once, to greet the Shabbat there! Would they all go with him?

But Jerusalem is very many miles away from Safed and his followers were dismayed. True, some of them responded at once to his entreaties, but they were few. The rest demurred, were faint-hearted, reluctant, and certainly could not go without first conferring with their wives . . . .

It was then that the great *ARI* was wracked with anguish and grief. All his being was overcome with suffering. For this, he knew, had been the acceptable hour for the Redemption; but the half-hearted cannot be redeemed. By their hesitation; their tarrying, their faltering courage, their shrinking unworthiness, their failure to meet the supreme test, they had let the blessed moment go by. The Exile must go on and on, unchanged. Where was the noble and unanimous purpose, the totally committed resolution to put away Sin and go up to the Spiritual Glory of Jerusalem, where all Israel would be redeemed; and where the Jewish heart and soul that would acclaim with one voice, that the Lord was One?

TO WELCOME QUEEN SHABBAT
IN JERUSALEM

The great ARI and his band of followers were preparing to welcome Queen Shabbat on the eve of her blessed approach. They were singing pious Psalms and Hymns as they strolled outside the City of Safed, already wearing the prescribed four white garments.

Tunefully, the Rabbi sang: "O come let us exult before the Lord! Let us shout for joy to the Rock of our Salvation . . . . O sing unto the Lord a new song; sing unto the Lord all the earth!" Then he changed to a sweet and tender melody: "Come my friends to meet the Bride! Let us welcome the Presence of the Sabbath . . . For it is a well-spring of blessing . . . ."

You have read the special and blessed experiences of the great sages and common people. May these beautiful words guide you and give you G-d's direction to happiness.

INDEX

About the Research Centre of Kabbalah

Kabbalah is mystical Judaism. It is the deepest and most hidden meaning of the *Torah*, or Bible. Through the ultimate knowledge and mystical practices of Kabbalah, one can reach the highest spiritual levels attainable. Although many people rely on belief, faith, and dogmas in pursuing the meaning of life, the unknown and the unseen, Kabbalists seek a spiritual connection with the Creator and the forces of the Creator, so that the strange becomes familiar, and faith becomes knowledge.

Throught history, those who knew and practiced the Kabbalah were extremely careful in their dissemination of the knowledge — for they knew the masses of mankind had not yet prepared for the ultimate truth of existance. Today Kabbalists know, through Kabbalistic knowledge, that it is not only proper but necessary to make available the Kabbalah to all who seek it.

The Research Centre of Kabbalah is an independent, non-profit institute founded in Israel in 1922. The Centre provides research, information, and assistance to those who seek the insights of Kabbalah. The Centre offers public lectures, classes, seminars, and excursions to mystical sites at branches in Israel — in Jerusalem, Tel Aviv, Haifa, Beer Sheva, Ashdod, and Ashkelon — and in the United States in New York and Los Angeles. Branches should soon be opened in Mexico City, Buenos Aires, Toronto, and Paris. Thousands of people have benefited by the Centre's activities, and the Centre's publishing of Kabbalistic material continues to be the most comprehensive of its kind in the world including translations in English, Hebrew, Italian, French, Russian, and Spanish.

Kabbalah can provide one with the true meaning of their being and the knowledge necessary for their ultimate benefit. It can show one spirituality which is beyond belief. The Research Centre of Kabbalah will continue to make available the Kabbalah to all those who seek it.

For additional information on the Centre, please contact (in the United States) Research Centre of Kabbalah International, 200 Park Avenue, Suite 303E, New York, N.Y. 10017; telephone (212) 986-2515 or (718) 805-9122.

"Love your fellowman as yourself."

According to the Kabbalah the universe resides in a system where an effect is a result of a cause which is indirect, but is neither random nor accidental. The root of this causality is imbedded in the creation and constitutes a passage to the physical realsm. Within the chain of "cause and effect" is found the life of man, and everything which happens in it. If man will see and understand this chain, he will know how to direct his life towards his goal through the easiest and best path, and will know to implement in a balanced way the love of his fellowman, as it is written, "Love your fellowman as yourself."

> ...[A]nd after forty days that the column will rise from the earth to the heavens in front of the eyes of the whole world the Mashiach will be revealed. From the East side a star will shine in surround this star and will make war with it from all the sides, three times a day for seventy days. And all the people of the world will see....
>
> —*Zohar,* 'Shemot' part 101

The Wisdom of Kabbalah and the Age of Aquarius
The wisdom of Kabbalah dates from thousands of years ago and has accompanied the world since its creation. The sages of Kabbalah have used its hidden knowledge in order to analyze and understand the reason for the universe and the reason for life. Today, in the age of Aquarius, the age of revelations and discoveries, this wisdom is being revealed to the public at large. The wisdom of Kabbalah, which is of "the ancient days", comes to develop whatever is found beyond the five senses of man, and reveals the tremendous forces which are hidden within him. It enlightens the miraculous harmony which exists in the universe and in our world, and directs each person to the harmonious path which is within his own life, and to the harmony which exists between himself and his fellowman.

The Answer to the Essence of Life
Kabbalah is the hidden knowledge of Judaism. Kabbalah sees in Judaism an expression of absolute perfection of the universe, not by

way of simply relating to the writings of Judaism in their external sense, but by penetrating to the very depth of truth. With the guidance of the book of Zohar written by Rabbi Shimon bar Yochai, it becomes possible for us to reach the essence of things, understand their roots, and directly reveal the solution to problems. Usually man relates to life within the framework of effects and results which are a collection of secondary branches, and which impede man's more basic, primary vision of the complete chain of events. The Kabbalah teaches us to see how the bridges are built between that which is in the Zohar concerning the past, present, and future, and the bridges upon which we have arrived today. The book of Zohar, with an intense light, illuminates the path which leads to the true solution of any problem from the most simple to the most complex.

"There is no question in the universe to which you will not find an answer in the teachings of Kabbalah," Rabbi Dr. P.S. Berg.

Courses Offered in the Research Centre of Kabbalah

It is the privilege of every man to reach the most elevated heights of understanding himself and the universe around him. The way to this understanding is through the teachings of Kabbalah. The Research Centre of Kabbalah presents courses in various fields of Kabbalah and studies in different levels of Zohar ranging from beginners to advanced levels. The following is a list of courses offered in the Research Centre of Kabbalah with a brief description of each course.

•*Kabbalah Basic Course*

This course includes the definition of terms and an introduction of understanding the principles of Kabbalah. It also includes concepts which are in effect the primary keys to the teaching of mysticism. This course represents an indispensable basis for the rest of the subjects which are taught in the Centre, even to the most advanced levels of Kabbalah studies.

•*Kabbalistic Meditation*

Kabbalistic meditation is a method of self-reflection dating from ancient days. It is based on the method of the previous Kabbalists and has been unified and simplified by the saintly ARI, Rabbi Yitzhak Luria, one of the great Kabbalists of Safed. This is a practical method which brings us to high levels of awareness and to the true evaluation of the forces which are hidden in man. Kabbalistic meditation acquires for us the tools necessary for bridging the gap between the forces of the soul and the forces of the body, and brings us to a growing utilization of the potential that is imbedded in us.

•*Reincarnation and Life After Death*

The Kabbalah sees in life not only a process of birth and death, but a continuous chain of cycles in which the soul (the inner energy of man) enters this world to fulfill a particular duty, and "leaves" it several times. The soul returns to the process of life many times in different bodies, up to the point where she reaches a perfect completion of the duty which has been assigned to her.

The understanding of this process leads to the understanding of all the processes which take place in the life of man. During his lifetime a man may ask himself who he is, why he was born to particular parents in a particular neighborhood; he is called by a name that was "fixed" for him and finds himself in a particular society to fulfill a particular duty. Why does he meet a particular spouse to bring into the world children with particular personalities and the like? There awaits to be revealed an amazing composition of a picture of a puzzle which when seen explains to us every instant of our lives, and also explains the historical process of life and the world, from its creation to its completion.